D0870618

Woman On Fire

by
Trinette Collier

FreedomInk
PO Box 1093 Reidsville, GA 30453

Copyright 2013 by Trinette Collier
All rights reserved. No part of this publication may be
reproduced or transmitted in any form or by any means,
electronic or mechanical, including photocopy,
recording, or any information storage and retrieval
system, without permission in writing from the copyright
owner.

Cover design by Elaina Lee.
Page layout by FreedomInk Publishing.
Final edit by Trinette Collier and
Katandra Shanel Jackson.

ISBN 978-0-9896786-2-9

Printed in the United States of America

www.freedomink365.com

To:
Felicia,
My sis,
thanks so
much 😊

Love

Tru

Special Thanks

A very special thanks is extended on behalf of the Author & Publisher, to all those that desired, did & will continue to support our literary efforts. Each cheer, well wish, dollar sowed, belief in the dream, makes all the difference. We truly appreciate the love & support from everyone... Especially you who have chosen to become *Angels of FreedomInk!* Thank you.

Latressa Crawford at Sensational Jireh Fashion Accessories & More

Yuma Mallard

Phillip Jackson

Dr. Darcova Triplett & The Ladies of STRUT!

Tangia Bowden

Yolanda Clay Triplett

Dawn Haynes

Damika McGuire

Shanay Benton

Cassandra Ollie

<u>DEDICATION</u>

Woman on Fire is dedicated to God… If it had not been for my trials and tribulations, I wouldn't have been this close to Him! I Thank You for my journey!

I love you forever and always!

Your daughter,
Trinette

<u>LETTER TO THE READER</u>

Dear Reader,

    'Woman On Fire' is a creative non fiction based on actual facts as the Author recalls them. *Names have been altered to protect the innocent and the not so innocent parties involved. Although these events did indeed happen in real life, 'Woman On Fire' is not history... It is *her*story!

    Out of the blazing flames of a personal inferno, a new creature will be born. We shall from hence forward call her woman.

    Dear Reader... please I implore you, enjoy the read!

Yours Truly,
Katandra Shanel Jackson,
CEO at FreedomInk Publishing
www.freedomink365.com

FOREWORD

Written by Legena M. Saxby Crawford

I have heard it said time and time again... "Where there is smoke there is fire." Fire has been contributed to numerous functions that we deem necessary for life; however, your encounter with it depends on your personal experience.

Fire has been used by humans for cooking, generating heat, signaling, and propulsion purposes. The negative effects of fire include water contamination, soil erosion, atmospheric pollution and hazard to life and property (Wikipedia). No matter what you use it for, fire has a purpose.

Woman on Fire is a compilation of all of the things that come along with what fire brings. What you are about to encounter is the true testimony of a woman who has experienced every level of fire known to man.

She has used it to cook meals for those who have eaten from her table and turned around to get up from the same table leaving her with dinner for one. She has used it to generate heat on cold nights while waiting for the one she loved to return the rubbing but not in the way she'd hope but instead, the rubbing that caused friction and not conviction. She has encountered fire used to signal for help when she didn't know which way to turn as the fire of life burned out of her control.

You will feel first hand the effects of life's encounters that caused water contamination as it polluted the well of life from which she drank. This pollution led to soil erosion that seemingly caused her to lose some ground sliding from the mountain top and avalanching into a valley of hurt, confusion, guilt, and shame.

As the years passed, the fire that was burning within began to seep through her soul resulting in atmospheric pollution as she was surrounded by the smoke and flames of her life that clouded her vision and caused her to feel that there was no way out. Family, friends and even God himself were looking for her as she hid in a closet of hurt and despair afraid to come out and walk through to the calls of those reaching out to give her the oxygen needed to restore her back to life.

From the view from the street, it looked as though this fire had burned out of control destroying everything in its path as is was hazardous to her life as the smoke almost literally choked her to death. However in the midst of the flames, she was able to use it to propel her into her purpose returning her to the God who created her. It was this God who knew where she was all the time as became to true firefighter of her soul breathing new life into her lungs.

You are invited to travel with me on the journey of a woman who had used the timbers of her soul to singe her the past and ignite her future.

TABLE OF CONTENTS

Special Thanks	5
Dedication	7
Letter to the Reader	9
Foreword	*11*
Prelude	17
Circa 1994 – 1998	29
Circa 1999	37
Circa 2000 – 2001	47
Circa 2002 - 2003	55
Circa 2004	63
Circa 2005	73
Circa 2006	89
Circa 2007	131
Circa 2008	177
Circa 2009	201
Circa 2010	213
Circa 2011	223
Circa 2012	229
Acknowledgements	239
Author Bio	247
Introduction to an Imprint	249
Also available at FreedomInk	251

<u>Woman on Fire Prelude</u>

The beginning of my journey started with the reading of Proverbs 31 and Esther, preparing to be a woman of God. Using these two books as a guide, my spiritual connection has begun to emerge. It was about seven years ago that my true spiritual transformation began. However, I had been connected with Jesus and the church since birth, through my parents and extended family.

I didn't frequent many churches. I had been a member of four denominations and attended about 4-5 churches; Baptist, Non-Denomination, United Methodist, African Episcopal Methodist (AME) and back to Non-Denomination. Each church and denomination served its purpose in my life and on this journey. I can't say which one was better because each church allowed me to connect with Him at different levels and at different stages.

Over the years, I visited churches but I was attending out of obligation to my grandparents, aunts/uncles, and friends who were members of churches. I wanted to belong. I had to belong and I felt left out. I was trying to be a church goer for the wrong reasons, for people, myself, but not for JC (Jesus Christ).

In 2002, I belonged to my ex-husband's church. Again, it was out of obligation and what I thought as being obedient to Christ. I followed my husband to start a new church 'career'. This was my plan; Me & him, with his parents, his generation of family members attending his church, going to church every Sunday, active, very impressive to his family... Blah, blah, blah. I assumed this was how my church path was supposed to be. I didn't know I was supposed to be spiritually connected because I was already on a church plan... My plan.

I continued to be active in church. I was the Director of Youth Ministry, Director of Outreach Ministry, Women's Day Chairperson, I volunteered for every committee. This was the Plan! I was on my way to becoming an integral part of the church family. I was a real church lady; the lady that would be pleasing to my families, the church people, my church going friends, and to Him upstairs. I had it all planned out. As I became more active, I wanted the Mr. to become more active as well. I began forcing him into going to church, which seemed crazy, after all it was HIS church! So why wouldn't he go? However, it didn't matter, my plan would work, after all, I am a church lady, right?

Ok, so moving right along. I'm connecting with 'church people', my family is happy because I'm able to stand and say "I first give honor to God, who is the head of my life. I bring to you greetings from blah-blah-blah-blah church under the pastoral leadership of the 'Rev. I Got A.Pasta' in Atlanta, Ga!" I had been practicing that speech and I was always ready to use it! I was high! High in church, high in the Lord! I had become Supa Christian!

Everything was going well. I had purchased our second home. I just became Teacher of the Year. I was still preparing for a baby. I was still active in church, community, and work. I was doing it! I was indeed Supa Christian. I couldn't be 'stopped'. Well, at least that's what I thought! 2005 was my year until something stopped me! I don't know what happened but it happened! Unexpectedly and without explanation, my feelings for my ex-husband started changing. My body was doing something, my mind was playing tricks on me, and more importantly, my spirit was being altered. No one in my circle understood what was going on. I went to the doctor whom was familiar with my medical history for the past 6 years, she said I was fine. Both my mother and mother-in-law said I was going through the mid 30's change. When I heard the word change, I immediately went into full throttle, baby mode! I had to get pregnant, like now! Because I was going through the change!!! So the mission was in place, I had to make this baby because I was changing and that was a bad thing for me. I'm in overdrive!

Spiritual cleansing was taking place and I didn't even know it. From 2005 to 2007, God had slowly taken over. My first stage of spiritual detox was hell! Literally. He was knocking the Hell out of me. Everything that was blocking my view of the Lord, He knocked them out of my life. He began to strip me... You can say I became a 'stripper' The first move was the church. I didn't have an interest in the church as a whole. That didn't mean I didn't love Him or the people of God. I just didn't like the feeling of obligation and the confinement of church. The walls were closing in on me. Everything about it became a question. A huge question mark lingered in that area of my life.

I began to question my beliefs, my morals, values, and past. I thought I was going to hell for real! I felt like I had denounced God because I didn't like church. Little did I know, this was the beginning of understanding the difference between being religious and spiritually connected. I began to stay away from church. Before I knew it, weeks turned into months with me dropping in every now & then just to get a Word.

I was now stripped of all the confusion of church. My mind was becoming free, free of traditional worship. So now, I'm free of church, step one. Now it was time for step 2 of the spiritual detoxification. Rid my sphere of distractions. This was the most painful part of the spiritual cleansing; job, marriage, home, car, finances, and the big one, INDEPENDENCE. Oh my Lord! He stripped me of it all! These were distractions that were hindering my true spiritual walk and I needed to be free so that I could hear Him.

Independence was mine!

But wait, oh my goodness, what the, are you serious JC? Really? You taking that away from me? What I did I do? Oh lawd, my life is over! My independence was just that, MINE! My momma gave it to me. My daddy gave it to me. My grandmamma, auntie, and my entire family gave me my independence and now He just swooped in and snatched it away! Just like that. I was not happy at all.

So here I am no money, no job, no residence, no car, no husband, and no more Ms. Independence. So what was I supposed to do? Jesus had gone OG, original gangsta on me. After all I had done for people, being good, being obedient to others, and more. I just knew God had finally gotten me. He was punishing me for losing my virginity (my parents/family stressed it!). He was punishing me for being unforgiving. He was punishing me for being mean and hateful towards others. Anything I did, God was punishing me for! When I say every negative thought came about, every and any thought entered my mind. What just happened to me?

I had to learn who my Heavenly Father was and this was the beginning of an amazing journey. After some much needed detoxing, spiritually, I began to 'see' Him. There was no more I, there was no more church, there was no more husband, family, or friends. It was just me and Him and I was scared as hell! I was entering into a new covenant that I knew nothing about. I felt alone, confused, angry, hurt, and sad. I couldn't understand why God was doing this to me. I was filled with questions of why?? Why You let my husband cheat? Why You didn't let me have a baby? Why You let me be embarrassed? Why? Why? Why Lord? Why am I becoming so distant from people? Why Lord? What did I do to You? At this point, I was beginning to talk to God, but this time, it was for real! You know how we do; when there's trouble, we become best friends with the Lord, Jesus Christ. But as soon as the rainbow appears, we get a little money in the purse, you and the bestie become a bit distant. However, this time it wasn't the case. It was me and Him all the way and I didn't know what to do.

This was my time to ask questions and seek answers. See, before, I was taught never to question God. You accepted whatever He is doing and you pray about it. Well, for me I started wondering and thinking, if I can't ask God then who am I going to ask? So being who I am, Ms. Questionnaire, I started asking everybody about what just happened, why was He doing this to me, and what do I do next, etc., etc., etc. I was completely consumed with asking questions and investigating what was His reasoning for sending a good person like myself through this hell. However, after months of questioning, no answers were given.

Like wow JC! You can't even answer me? So then I began to rethink the whole concept of me not supposing to ask Jesus questions. As I lay in bed, totally depressed, sad, and angry, I cried my heart out. I slowly began to feel something, it felt different. I felt Him... Finally. Everything is gone. All of the distractions. It was just 'You and Me' (singing Tony! Toni! Toné!). I had no choice but to get to know my new man, my Heavenly Father. It was time to learn how to be a woman of God.

Woman On Fire

by
Trinette Collier

Circa 1994-1998

Woman on Fire
Circa 1994-1998

And in the beginning there was...

I was living with a stranger. How could this be? I didn't know who I was anymore. I didn't know what I liked, who I liked, what I wanted, where I wanted to be or what I wanted to be. The walls were closing in on me. I became withdrawn into my inner self. Hiding from the world. I wasn't vibrant anymore. I was dull, convenient, and predictable. I was complacent. I wasn't me. My circle of friends noticed how clingy I had become. They noticed that I was desperately trying to make them happy. I couldn't afford for anyone else to leave me.

Prior to this life changing experience, the death of my dad in 1994 altered my world. I never thought of my parents leaving me, not even dying. Every child's thought is that your parents live forever and I continued to believe that. When he died, he left me and I felt empty. So I had to fill that void and I did so by getting married. Only to fill the void and provide security and company of a male companion. I never healed from his untimely death.

Over a period of time I fell into a bleak depression. I planned how long my healing would take and mapped out how I would overcome the grief and pain of his death. Because I didn't know who I was and I didn't care about life anymore, I began dating a few men. Honestly, I didn't date... I gave myself away to men controlling my feelings with them. I was like the dude in a relationship. I would pick one, hit it, and leave no traces of me ever being around.

Quiet as it was kept, you never knew that this college educated, Christian, church going, obedient, family & friends pleasing, always smiling girl was in tragic pain. It was a pain that I couldn't describe because I had never felt like this ever. I didn't understand why God took my dad away from me and my family so I somewhat stopped believing. I became rebellious in my Christian walk. Not forsaking Him but I wanted to hurt God like He hurt me. I wasn't going to live for Him anymore.

From 1994 until 1998, I lived multiple lives. It wasn't reckless. I wasn't a prostitute, stripper, gambler, alcoholic, or any of that. I was a daughter, a sister, a granddaughter, a niece, a cousin, a co-worker, a friend, a college graduate, a new teacher, and more. But I was never Trinette LaShon Collier. I had a set of Christian friends & family that said I couldn't do this, couldn't do that, I had to look a certain way, wasn't supposed to enjoy life, had to stay in the bible to prove that I knew Jesus, etc. Then I had a set of 'regular ole folk' who loved life. Secretly I was attracted to the 'regular ole folk' and I was always torn between both worlds. I could hang but I couldn't... I tried to smoke, drink, cuss, cheat, steal, lie, have sex and more... it would never work out!

I took my first drink after graduating college! I lost my virginity in college at 21! So I was totally a late bloomer according the world. I couldn't live wrong when I tried! If I lied, you would know because I would end up confessing that I lied! I remembered planning to get drunk and just letting it all out... well, that didn't go so well because I got drunk off some cheap brown liquor and started running my mouth not realizing I was talking way too much! In reality, I was confessing that I was having hidden sex with many men and I was ashamed!

Since I was from California, South Central to be exact, I tried to prove to folks that I was down and I could hang. I was trying to create a cool person with a flair of drama. It created drama alright! I tried to smoke Black & Milds and joints along with drinking. What the hell! Who in the hell don't know how to roll a joint and puff? Me! That's who!!! I couldn't even roll a joint let alone smoke it! The people put me in my own corner and told me NOT to move because I was going to ruin their high! That's how 'out of place' I was!

That wasn't even the half of it. For years people recognized that I had a special calling on my life. I didn't see it however. There was a dear friend name Charles, God rest his soul, who would call me Sistah Kate all the time! I would get mad because he made me sound like a misfit by saying, "That's just who you are! You are not supposed to be hanging with us! Sistah Kate, you just don't belong!" And he was right, I didn't belong. I was living multiple lives trying to fit in. I'm glad those days were short! That would be another book entitled, The Mishaps of the Misfit! But please don't get it twisted, they did call me the Quiet Storm and I could get down with the get down... if need be. I was looked at sideways for a long time because I became a hypocrite. So, therefore, I had to prove to people who I was again!

Circa 1999

Woman on Fire
Circa 1999

In 1999, my sister was getting married and that wasn't cool, in my book. That meant she would leave me and cling to her soon to be husband. I wouldn't have any one to chit chat with or fuss and fight with; we're known to be a mixture of the Headabrinks & MaryMary. Besides, I was the oldest and I was supposed to get married first. The feeling of being lonely was elevating to the next level and that couldn't happen. Again, someone else that I loved was leaving me so I had to do something quick, fast, and in a hurry! I was determined NOT be alone. So, let the interview process begin!

I had been in a steady but unhealthy relationship throughout my college years, so having an adult relationship would be different. I knew what I wanted in a man. I knew I needed someone I could control simply because I had been controlled for too long! What did Janet say? Control... I felt what she was saying! In the next year, I had started on a quest to find myself a husband. Reason number 1, I was about to hit the 30 year mark and in woman term, that was tragic if you were not married by 30! Reason number 2, I wanted to have unlimited sex without being condemned. Reason number 3, I wanted a child and I knew I needed a husband and last but not least, reason number 4, I didn't want to be alone. As I was interviewing for potential husbands I completely put the death of my dad in the back of my mind. I was losing focus on dealing and healing, so I chose to cover pain with getting married. After reading all of the popular self-help books at that time, I thought I had dealt with my inner feelings but all the while, I was still covering up a lot! I entered a relationship! It was happening! I'm gonna be married y'all!

Going into 2000, a new decade, I'm in the zone! I'm getting closer to turning 30 years old and I want to be married, I need to be married, I GOT to be married! That was the only way I could have my baby. I needed my own person to love and I didn't want to be alone. I wanted someone who would be with me forever and ever... No matter what! I needed a baby! I began to slowly bury all of my hurt and pain and denial of my father's death away; so far away that I honestly thought my dad would come home soon. Yes, I lost it, but no one knew it because I was a careered woman, an educated woman, a Christian woman, a sister, daughter, friend, cousin, colleague, co-worker, etc... I was everything to everyone except me. I didn't know who I was. For twelve years, I didn't know me...That's a long time to be lost! So I needed to speed up these interviews!

Candidate #1

He wasn't my 'type' but he was financially stable; an older, nice looking gentleman. He belonged to a national organization, so he was quite active in community service. We had sex and there was no connection other than me being released. We never talked about anything. He moved backwards, he had sex with me THEN he wanted to get to know me. I played the role of a man, had sex and then wanted him out of my space. On a scale of 1-5, he was a 3. No passion or romance and he had a teenage child! I was too young to be a stepmom to a teenager. Chile, he was heartbroken that I didn't want see him anymore. Oh well... Next!

Candidate #2
This young man was in and out of my life over the years. So we had a better relationship. We became friends but I don't think it was really a friendship because he too was searching to be loved by one woman. Two emotional people don't need to get together! No ...don't need two people crying! Of course we had sex quite often and he fell 'in love' with me. I wasn't. He was nice, funny, sensitive, kind and very willing to be with me. No children, no previous relationship drama. So why didn't I connect with him? He was too emotionally unstable and I truly didn't need that. Hell, I was already grieving! Next!

Candidate #3
This was it! This was my husband to be! I met his parents, they liked me and I liked them. Tall, handsome, funny, cool as hell. We were cool. I was even willing to

compromise my standards and become a stepmom to his two & half kids (he didn't know if one was his or not). We had a long distance relationship but we saw each other every week. Of course, we had sex quite often because we were in a serious relationship. We were going pretty strong until it was time for me to visit him one spring break. After confirming I was on my way, (leaving from work), this Negro left me a message, "Oh, I don't think we should chill this week, I'm seeing somebody else." Scooby Doo pause! What in the hell! So of course I cried for a minute and then the famous woman syndrome kicked in! Yall know that syndrome... When we get pissed over a man, we get that eff'em courage! And that's what I did! I didn't care! Negro, you want to play with my heart and feelings after I let you into my world! It's like that?! You must be eff'n crazy! Yep, I was in my zone and that wall went back up!!

So Candidate #3 broke my already broken heart, but it created an even thicker shell. A wall so tough and strong no one and I mean no one would ever get through it... Never again. I could go down the list of the flaws but I won't...that's not me anymore. Moving on... Next!

Candidate #4

Bam! Boom! Bahdow! I got'em! I found my husband! Yes, this was it and I could move forward with my plans! But Candidate #3 now wanted to come back into my life... Really? Candidate #4 arrives on the scene. Young, cute, vibrant, and the one, I could handle. Didn't need to interview him because he seemed right. He came from a two parent home, 'stable', no children, in school to further his education, goal oriented and did I mention that he was cute? Wrapped packages can be very deceiving!

Stop the press! He was hired! I met him in September, I opened my life to him, we got engaged in December, he moved in my crib in February, I bought a house in August 2000; we married in the house in January 2001 and had the actual ceremony that following April. What a year! That is what Grands would call a shotgun wedding. The difference? I wasn't pregnant, I was just trying to get pregnant. There was no time at all to get to know this brother. I met my goal of being married by 30. Yes I did, yes I did! I ran that marathon, quick, fast and in a hurry! I went from Miss to Mrs. in record time! He was hired and I's married now!

So, I literally had gone through four men within one years' time. I had become addicted to finding love but used sex to find it. I had sex first then learned about the person afterwards. I didn't think I was a jezebel, harlot, hoe, etc... because I was a good girl, I used protection each time, I loved the Lord and I kept it classy! I never got gifts or things paid for, money in the account, rent paid, nothing. I didn't want anything but a husband. All the while as I lay up with these men pondering if they could be my husband or not. Nothing else mattered. I had to have a man because my time was running out. Of the 13 men that I was sexually active with during my adult years, there were only 4 possible Candidates that could fulfill my request and meet my standards. Out of all these men, not one could do it for me! The reality of my life was that I really didn't have any standards! What was really going on?

Circa 2000-2001

Woman on Fire
Circa 2000-2001

Stop the Press! Stop the Press! I found my husband! Notice I said, 'I found my husband!'? It was Labor Day weekend in 2000 and my girls and I were hanging out in a popular Buckhead area. I was feeling good, looking good, had money in my account, riding around in a newly purchased SUV and it was a 3 day weekend so I was ready to have some fun! We rolled around the block, got out and walked. You know the scene; everybody out, having a good time. I could stay out as late as I wanted to, I did not have to answer to anybody. I was totally free.

That's when I saw him! This tall, big dude! Cute baby like face, nice teeth with a nice smile. Don't worry, I am NOT, I repeat, I am NOT having a fond flashback!!! Matter of fact, as I'm writing this, I'm thinking to myself, 'What in the HELL was I thinking!!!' I am seeing ALL OF THE RED FLAGS... A decade later!

Moving right along. Needless to say, we exchanged numbers and that Negro spent the entire Labor Day weekend with me. I admit, at that time it was nice to have a friend. We talked and talked and instantly became a 'couple' after chilling with each other for 3 whole days! He expressed how I was cool and I expressed how he was cool, etc...etc...etc...WHATEVER! All the while we were chillin, I'm still thinking, I can control this one, but he wanted to stay around! How was I going to get rid of him? I was still seeing someone else and was really hoping that the other one would come around but this Negro won my heart! So, instantly, he and I became 'boyfriend and girlfriend' in September, literally!

I never dated my ex-husband so I didn't see anything 'wrong'. Honestly, I knew there was something wrong but it didn't matter because I had the money, I had the residence, I had my career and if I needed to do for myself, I could and I did! So I didn't need him for anything except to lie in my bed. I could rightfully say I have a husband, not a man, but a husband.

The signs were there that I shouldn't have even remotely got involved with him. Where should I start?

1. No car
2. Still lived with parents
3. No steady job
4. No career goals…had them but not focused enough
5. No money
6. He saw me as an opportunity
7. Bad credit
8. No stability
9. Family issues
10. Just plain wrong for me

But like I said, it didn't matter because I had it under control. I just wanted to have a husband so I could have unlimited sex and make a baby before 31. Remember, I had to get married before 30 so I had planned on being pregnant by 31 with my first child. He knew my plan and was down with it because he wanted the same thing. Everything I wanted he wanted too! Really? Really! By December he had asked me to marry him. He asked my mother for her permission, which I thought was nice but it didn't matter to me. He didn't have a ring but it was ok. He worked hard to get me a nice diamond by the time our nuptials took place. Yes, it was very nice! No complaints in that department. In fact, I give him kudos for having such great taste in jewelry.

I accepted his proposal and began pulling out my preplanned wedding book! Ladies, you know that Pre-Wedding book of your future! I was excited because I was getting married and all before 30! He wanted to get married within 6 months and I wasn't ready for that! We played 'house' when I gave him a key for Valentine's Day! Mistake! His bills now became a burden because I was debt free. I had the basic bills... Georgia Power, Clayton County Water, Isuzu, Gieco and a handful of a few more small, manageable bills were mine! DAMN, DAMN, DAMN!!! I miss those days! Seventy-nine cent gas at the QT!

We set the date for a spring wedding, April 2001, but it was pushed back because I decided I wanted to buy a house. I was ready to buy one but I wanted to buy it with my husband, however, it was my money that would make the purchase. So from January until June, I was planning a wedding and house hunting. Still yet to date and really get to know him. I never knew his dislikes, his needs, wants, desires, goals or his family history... None of that! I just saw a cute, 6'4 Negro who could make me a baby.

Let's recap; I met him in September, we got engaged in December and shacked up in February, I bought our first home in August, and we married in the home in January of 2001! Who did I marry? The hell if I know!

Circa 2002-2003

Woman on Fire
Circa 2002-2003

They call me Mrs....
He was so cute! He was all into me! I was the wife and he knew it! I cooked, cleaned and sexed! To him it seemed as if I had a substantial amount of money, and I did but it was due to years of savings that was not to be touched! I was in marital bliss. Whatever he did, it was cute and cool. His clothes hanging all over the place? It was ok because he was cute and he was my husband. I was happy! Dirty towels in the tub? It's ok, that's my husband. I was happy! Money missing from my accounts? Girl, that's ok, he got a good reason besides he's sooo cute and he's my husband! And I was happy! Nothing was wrong. For the first four years, I lived in my own fantasy world of how a marriage was supposed to be.

You want to hear how 'Happily Ever After' really played out in my mind? Here it goes; I was supposed to cook, clean, sex, bear children, plan & organize family time, take care of hubby, sit on the PTA, participate in all the church functions, bake, provide care for everyone, still have my career and still look fabulous! WHEW! Oh, I forgot, it was also my responsibility to entertain friends! Yes that was my 'goal'. I was the picture perfect Christian woman! I thought that was the life. I was completely wrong! Somehow, I was born too late because I swear this was a woman of the 50s trapped in a woman of the 2000's.

The first four years were really great! My exterior boasted that I was extremely happy but I was actually sad inside. His parents said we were still in the honeymoon phase. We were somewhat in sync (really we were not... but it seemed as though). We were living the life of a newly married couple. We were hanging out, even dressing similar on occasion. Attending games, going to church, hanging with new friends and family, hosting gatherings; all the stuff that a girl dreams of doing with her man. He was in & out of jobs as he tried to complete his education but I didn't mind because he said that he had me, meaning he would soon pick up the ball and be the man of the house, financially, and I was still happy!

We had discussed having children so that plan was in the making. He wanted to start a family and so did I. But I knew I couldn't quite start a family just yet because I was in school receiving my Masters and it was hard enough adjusting to being married. I did have that much sense to say let's wait. However, I started preparing my body physically for a baby, not mentally or spiritually but physically. The pressure was already on from his father. He wanted to know why I hadn't gotten pregnant yet, it had been four years already... Sorry Pops. I hate to tell you but I ain't like the other women. Houston, we got a problem! Although we didn't have any children yet, we were still happy and going strong. I was happy! With determination, I was going to be a mother, soon and very soon!

Woman on Fire
Circa 2002-2003

Here comes the heat…

I had been trying to have a child since we got married in 2001. We started the process which was simple, have sexual intercourse during your peak times of ovulation and boom, I would become pregnant! Well, that didn't quite take place for me. For a while, it didn't bother me that I hadn't become pregnant. My sex drive was extremely high… I mean like a dog in heat! I had to have it all day and every day so I didn't know why I couldn't conceive. I was just excited that I would be pregnant soon. I didn't know anything was wrong until later in our marriage.

By this time, I was starting to believe the previous doctor when he said I would never conceive. So I became discouraged each time my period came. I had so many home pregnancy tests in my bathroom that if one of my friends discovered they needed one, they didn't have to go to to the local pharmacy, they just got one from me!

I took a pregnancy test every month, and month after month, nothing. That is the saddest and most painful feeling ever when you're on a journey of trying to become a mother. That excitement of the possibilities of being pregnant, creating cravings, mentally thinking your body is changing once you miss the first day of your cycle. It's hard to come down off that excitement when everyone is excited that you're excited and waiting. So I started asking my doctor about my body and why I wasn't conceiving. She began to give me natural & medical remedies on top of remedies. I could have written a book on the remedies alone! She told me to relax, she told me make sure to lie still after sex, take liquid Geritol, and more. And like an anxious child, I did them all faithfully.

I followed the temperature chart, charting my cycles and all that jazz. I lay in different positions after sex, hoping the sperm would swim to its destination. I remember after doing my wifey duty, I would lay upside down with my legs up on the wall for about an hour! My goodness! My legs got numb! Then there were times I would place pillows under my pelvic area after sex, just lying there asking him NOT to touch me! Sex became a task. It became loveless and unenjoyably and stressful. Each moment was not about my mate, it was about making a baby. I timed the sex, day, night, in between, I was in 'heat'... Not for him but for the standard biological ticking clock. Lawd, have mercy! All of these positions were crazy! Not saying they don't work but it was crazy! I would pray, read, rub my belly with 'holy oil', finding scriptures that were tailored for me and all that stuff. I was a believer because He said I would be a mother! Hmmm... That's what I heard! Mrs. Trinette Collier Lewis* was finally going to be a mother.

Circa 2004

Woman on Fire
Circa 2004

I opened a savings account with the baby's name. I had chosen a girl's name because it was prophesized to me that I would have a girl! So I started buying cute dresses, hair bows, and onesies. I made the mistake of telling people about the fertility process. I expected people to be happy and positive. Some thought I was crazy for buying things and preparing her room. Some thought the idea of prophesy was a religious hoax. And some became afraid that I would become that woman who would do anything to get a baby. Sad but true.

So my faith kicked in because it was happening! I started believing in this dream simply because I saw the process. I was reading my Bible more, pulling scriptures to assist me and praying more. I was really praying. I didn't prepare the room due to the fact that we were moving. The plan was to find a house with additional space, great neighborhood, good school district and a quality environment for our children. I traded in my small Honda Civic for a Chevy Trailblazer so the car seats could fit. I didn't create any bills because I was building the savings account and buying savings bonds for her future. My finances were good.

I started eating healthier, detoxing, relaxing, and keeping the excitement going! I created her first journal with pictures of her mommy and daddy. I signed up for every baby magazine, parenting magazine, giving potential due dates to get freebies at events, trying on maternity clothes, and all! I had become obsessed with making this baby. I wanted to be pregnant and I wanted to be pregnant now.

Woman on Fire
Circa 2004

So here it is, 2004. I received my Masters of Education, that meant pay increase! I wanted another home because the neighborhood wasn't really what the city had said it would be. So, we were on the hunt for a new home and we started the Baby Chronicles. That was the most exciting time for me. I was settling into the marriage, still excited and happy about him. Still excited about having a child or two. I was thinking ahead about our future and not seeing the signs of potential disaster.

He started telling a few lies here & there about finances. That should have raised a brow but being in love can blind you. He was forgiven and I overlooked his transgressions. We started talking about having a baby, so I made my appointment with my wonderful OB/GYN to discuss my body. I was nervous because prior to that, I had a doctor to tell me that due to a condition I had, I would never conceive.

So they placed me on meds and told me that I had a choice to either get the tumor removed or stay on the meds for the rest of my life. I thought about the operation but opted out and wanted to stay on the meds. The doctor was dry and to the point. He stripped my womanhood away when he gave me that 'option' and that stuck with me forever. After praying, God sent me a new doctor (whom I stayed with for 6 years). This was the start of an exciting but scary journey. I was actually going to become a mother! So the journey begins!

I started going to the doctor, they were running test, all kinds of test. On me and then him, but the excitement was still there because I thought I was getting closer. It was four years later so I knew my time was coming. Besides the Lord promised me that I would have children so it had to happen... Right? I created a Baby T journal. It was cute and dear to me. I placed all of the doctor's appointments and remedies in it. A picture of both me and my baby daddy and other family members; I was speaking life into my unborn child. I was happy!

Woman on Fire
Circa 2004

The house hunt was going well. The first house, we placed a down payment on it but the builder collapsed so after 6 months we were looking for another. I wasn't worried but getting anxious because I needed to continue to be stress free. So the baby making plans continued. After a few months of testing, they decided to put me on Clomid which would ultimately help me conceive. I was so excited about being on medication that it was insane! Only because I knew other women who were on it and they conceived after a few dosages.

So, the doctor prescribed the Clomid and I was excited about being on this medicine. I really shopped and ran my mouth! I had about 3 pocket calendars on deck! Circling, highlighting, abbreviating, all of it! I timed it. By 2005, I would be pregnant and wearing the latest & cutest maternity wear out there! I was determined to be the cutest pregnant woman, representing for the over 30 moms and still able to keep my sexy. I was so ready! I signed up to have a Doula; I didn't discuss it with him, but I had also signed up for birthing classes. I was extremely confident and excited! I was ready to be a mom... Finally!

Woman on Fire
Circa 2004

The summer of 2004 was coming to a close and I still wasn't pregnant... Yet. However, we finally closed on our 2nd home! We were finally moving into our new dream family home. The home where I would start my family and create the 'TV'/fairytale book memories. It was all coming together, my plan.

The home was what I asked for. Ranch style home with three bedrooms, a perfect sitting space for the baby's room, full basement stubbed & ready for 4 more rooms where I could house my business. Large front yard and a decent backyard. Nice deck to host parties, family reunions and my girls nights. Entertaining friends and family was essential, so the kitchen was on point, it was spacious! Sidewalk community, HOA, variety of neighbors, good school district, and it was new! Everything had a warranty! No fixing up, no repairs! My scent and only scent in this brand new family home, Yes, Lord! Thank you! You are blessing me! I'm sorry Lord for being so mad with You but...

I was getting close! Real close to completing my storybook moment! Welcome to Our Home!

Circa 2005

Woman on Fire
Circa 2005
It's a New Season....

Moving, unpacking, meeting neighbors, heading back to work happy and still not pregnant, but I was ok because the plan was coming together! By this time, the Clomid wasn't being as effective as the doctor wanted it to be so the next step was IVF, in vitro fertilization. It was time to see a Specialist.

I wasn't too knowledgeable about this process at first. I thought the doctor was suggesting getting a donor! And I was literally considering it but my husband wasn't having it! So, after being educated on IVF, we were set to go. I was desperate! I was excited! I gave the OK to start! So we went through the informational session in the upcoming weeks. However, the doctor wanted me to continue the Clomid another round which I thought was odd because it didn't work the previous time. However, they were the specialists and I was excited, so let's do this! To God be the

Glory! This woman on fire was spiritually anxious.

Woman on Fire
Circa 2005

The time had come when my Ob/Gyn referred me to a fertility specialist because I had developed Type II Diabetes. Get the &%# out of here... Are you serious? Something else is blocking me from having this baby! First the tumor in the base of my brain that is preventing me from ovulating and now this shit! God, why are you doing this to me? All I want is a baby! A damn baby! Now I'm going to be on meds on top of meds. This is some bullshit! The other women I know didn't have to go this, so why I am I having to do this?

Being a school teacher, I saw countless parents coming in & out with bellies popped out with their 3rd, 5th, and even 12th child! So why in the hell couldn't I be like that? The anger and frustration started to set in. Besides, this is not fair! I go to church every Sunday, well, I missed some Sundays because I had games to attend or events to do or parties to host.

Lord, I'm paying my tithes after I shop for friends and family or go on trips... I politely give you what I have left. I am praying Lord... When I get the time to really pray, I pray and read my scriptures. You've blessed me so much so why are you doing this to me? I don't understand it! I waited to get married to consider having a baby, I've been following you and you promised me! So what's wrong? I thought you said you forgave me of all of my past sins! Something ain't right and it's not cool. I'm just saying...Dammit, I'm a Christian woman and I'm supposed to get what I pray for... You 'IS' trippin'!

Woman on Fire
Circa 2005

By this time, I was doing my best to stay hopeful because I was going to the best fertility clinic in Atlanta. I made the appointment for a consultation; might I add, this process was not only tedious but at $300 per office visit, very expensive! During the consultation I was asked a lot of preliminary questions such as, "How long have you been trying to conceive?" "Are there any women in your family who've had trouble conceiving?" "What's your diet?" "We will need for you to lose more weight." The questions were so overwhelming that I just sat there and almost said forget it... I don't want no damn child! This is too ga'damn hard! Why am I praying and what am I praying for! I mean like for real. The bible said to ask and I will receive!

My then husband, whom was very supportive, continued to encourage me throughout the process. Then after the consultation, we had to come back for tests! Blood tests, egg and sperm count test, any other tests. They came back to only say that it was him with a low sperm count and my eggs were good. That was the first initial round of test. So then I was ok with that. They gave him strategies to increase his count. It wouldn't take long so I was getting excited! We just had to stay on the doctor's plan and work it!

Woman on Fire
Circa 2005

I've always been a child of God but I was introduced to Jesus when I was a child through my grandmother, mom and great aunt, then my father came aboard later in life. They were strong believers and worshippers. My life was given to Him in church at an early age. As stated earlier, I can remember the number of churches that I've been a member of and each one served its purpose in my life. But my spiritual transformation began in 2005 and it was a good year!

I was married since 2001 and we had just purchased our second home. It was a total upgrade from my first place. A $250,000, 3 bedrooms, 2 full baths, huge kitchen, living room, sun-room, deck, land, and a full basement ranch. Great school system, new community, sidewalks, HOA (Home Owners Association)... It was THE house for us and I was proud and happy. I was praising God, now! I was happy again! He had BLESSED me and I was back at being my 'happy' self, but still, there was no full commitment to Him. For a minute, I forgot about the baby journey. I kept a tab of every dollar spent, not to showboat, but as a reminder of how proud I was to be able to make such purchases even after a few credit challenges. I knew it was all God!

2005 was a good year for me. I still wasn't pregnant but I was getting close because God had blessed me/us with the 'dream' family home to start a family. So I was cool with that. I was happy at work because I received Teacher of the Year award for my school and I was happy! My husband was settling in because he finally found his new career and I was good! I started asking him was he ready to take his role as head of household because I was ready to leave my profession. Prior to this when we first met, I told him that I wanted to be a stay at home mom & work my business. He said that he would have my back and to go for it.

So, he was working, I'm working, still saving, still planning. The fertility process was starting to go as planned. My eggs were ready to be penetrated. I was in baby mode! I had begun preparing for motherhood, again. But this time, my life was really 'perfect'. I was faithfully taking both meds, eating right, exercising, losing the weight, praying more, going to church a bit more. I was believing more because I could see my blessings. I was finally 'right' with the Lord… I had gotten back to my spiritual roots. The truth is, I had become spiritually bipolar.

Woman on Fire
Circa 2005
It's My Season

I had started my first business which was California Dreaming Events Planning, Inc. Yes, chile, I had to add that INC. in it to make it official! I was co-founder of another business with my friend/partner. These plans were discussed with my husband prior (like 4 years prior), so I was good! I also started his massage therapy business as a birthday present to him. I took my tax refund and found a small space for his clients. I enlisted a few friends to help me surprise him, painted, shopped for all of the equipment (and that stuff ain't cheap) and created the cutest but manly Massage Therapy space ever! I remember my nail stylist was like "Wow! You are truly a sincere and good wife!" Those words validated me because I did something 'perfect'.

Yes! I believed in my husband and I was going to make him have a business, income, and more. He said he wanted it so I honored his wish, that's what a wife is supposed to do, correct? I was so excited for him and me and us! He was finally going to be able to support me, the baby, and be the head of the house. But my then husband was in his own world and I could feel it, but it didn't matter because God had answered my prayers and was still answering them. Checking off my desires one by one from the list of 'Lord, I want this, I want that, I need this, and oh, I need that!' Family was good, friends were good, church was good....! I had consulted with the husband to make sure everything was cool and to make sure he was prepared for me to leave education to work the businesses full time. It didn't matter anyhow, because I had a plan! September 2005 was a good year!

I was happy! I had my husband, my family, my friends, my soon to be pregnancy, my career, my home, my businesses, my plans, and my god.....I spy with my natural almond shaped brown eye, something was out of order. But I swear fo gawd 2005 was a good year!

Woman on Fire
Circa 2005

Did I mention that 2005 was a good year? It was one of many good years. Money was good and all. The fall of 2005 was really cool. That November, my birthday was really great! He considered the house as my gift for me. The Teacher of the Year ceremony had taken place across the district and I was extremely happy with that outcome as well. Things were really going good. I was honored because I was finally validated in my career. It had been one of my goals... I excelled in my career and esteemed achievement was on my Life Plan.

I was still trying to get pregnant, still on the meds. The Type 2 Diabetes were now under control so I pretty much weaned myself off that nasty medication. I was still exercising with a trainer who also knew I was trying to conceive. We were settling in the house. But I didn't want to cover the walls just yet with beautiful art or pictures or decorate. In this big home, I had one sofa that had been kept on display in the furniture store like forever; one television (his), a very inexpensive kitchen table & chairs, no complete bedroom suite, just a bed and night tables. I had complete kitchen ware and bathroom sets and even my office furniture, but our home still felt incomplete.

The house was clean, immaculate. You could literally eat off the floors. The smell was fresh, crisp, and clean. I lived for a clean and neat home. Matching towels and sheets were freshly washed, dried and folded a particular way. I used certain brands of washing powder and all of its side kicks, faithfully. Dishes were washed in bleach, dried, and organized in the cabinets in decent order. The food pantry was grocery store organized to the max. The fridge was also stocked like the grocery store. The daily clean-up of the kitchen consisted of washing the dishes in bleach hot water, dried, put away, wipe down the stove, microwave, counters, refrigerator (inside & out), sweep and mop the floor… good night. No dishes in the sink! Carpet was vacuumed every day…

Errrrrday and dare not walk with shoes on it. Bathrooms were sparkling clean. Any dirt, I immediately cleaned on the spot. Closets were stocked with rolls of tissue, soap, and the necessities. There were no excuses for us to run out of anything. My walls were white on white except the kitchen. Apple green paint specially mixed from the local home store. The colors were to be apple red and green. The guest bedroom had a complete bedroom set but that room was off limits and used for family guest or friends. Explanation... There would be no reason for him to say that I didn't keep a clean house! I was OCD to the highest power! I kept clutter to a minimum. The less I had in the house, the cleaner it would stay. Even the junk in the basement was organized. I just had to keep a 'perfect' home. A perfect home that I didn't enjoy living in. I was silently disturbed.

Circa 2006

Woman on Fire
Circa 2006
Smoke signals...

Things started shifting for me, for us. In my world, things were going great but in the 'real world', things were starting to burn. I saw the signals but was in denial. The baby making process was becoming frustrating and wasn't fun anymore. I became depressed and angry at the fact that I couldn't conceive like other women. By now, it was approaching the 5th year of me trying to conceive. It seemed as though everybody I knew was popping up pregnant, some with their first child and others with additional children.

I was going to all the baby showers, giving baby showers and nothing was for me. At some showers, I would fake the funk of happiness and at others I didn't care; I still kept hope alive. I was even jealous of other women. YES, this good Christian woman was J-E-A-L-O-U-S! Sitting there, shower after shower, silently praying and asking God why can't this be me? Thinking about what is wrong with my body. People still asking when we were going to have children and having to say it with a smile... "Soon yall, very soon. We're working on some things." Or I would say "Chile I ain't trying to have no kids right now, I got business to tend to." I would lie in public but I was screaming inside with anger.

At this point, I would even pray to get pregnant and didn't mind if I miscarried or not. I was still taking meds and they were trying to decide on the IVF treatment. I was excited not thrilled, but at least it was a chance. The visits to the doctors became a routine and sex was a task. Scheduling sex time was the new normal. What was once fun and spontaneous now became a tedious task that required an appointment according to my temperature and mood. Love making was no longer inviting and I didn't look at him as my husband anymore. I was so focused on getting his sperm and I was determined to do so. This was my daily routine; work, home, cook, wait for him, let's do it, plan for baby, go to sleep anxiously, start over the next day.

I became obsessed with perfection. Everything had to be just right. I had to make sure we had sex in the right positions. After sex, I would lay in unconventional positions, making sure that his sperm would poke something! I talked about babies all day and all night! I wasn't happy anymore and I felt like he failed me and I failed myself but I was determined to keep trying, no matter what!

Woman on Fire
Circa 2006
Prophecy of A New Year...

There was a beautiful and perfect sitting area in the master bedroom. We agreed to make that Baby T's room. She gave me the name that was given to her for me to name the baby but I didn't like it. So I continued to call her by the name I had chosen, which was a combination of his & mine... Classic! Being disobedient cost me. She never said when I would conceive her but that I would have a baby girl. I believed my aunt because she is a believer and a praying woman of God so I started speaking to my stomach daily. Anointing my belly and speaking to my womb every day. I had begun preparing the nursery, setting up her bank account, shopping for baby furniture and clothes. I had a seamstress to create Mother & Daughter dresses.

Her name began to be part of my daily conversation. I had already written it many times throughout the years. I had become obsessed with having her. She was my life but no one knew it. I thought about how she would be, what she would be like, her smell, her eyes, nose, mouth, etc... I tried to imagine his genes and mine together. I dreamed about her but could never see her face. I could never get to that point of knowing her. I never got a chance to meet her.

I believed, I believed, and I believed. Faithfully and conveniently trusting God and reading the scriptures on faith. I was listening to others about how my time was coming. It was all starting to overwhelm me but I was determined to have a child, soon. 2005 wasn't over yet so it could still happen. Why Lord? Why didn't You give me my daughter that You promised! I don't believe you anymore... You don't love me anymore... I am hurt... I am sad... I'm not happy.
Happy New Year.......

Woman on Fire
Circa 2006

By spring of 2006, I was sitting on the couch, no TV, no radio, no phone, just sitting, looking at the bare white walls. One day I was just sitting when he walked into the living room, I burst into tears! He ran over and asked what was wrong? I just remember crying and lying on his lap telling him that he was not doing right! I didn't know what I was talking about... I didn't understand why this message was coming out of my mouth but I knew something wasn't right and my now ex-husband was pretending it was. Almost every day, I cried. I woke up crying, in the middle of teaching, I cried, cooking and crying, crying myself to sleep, just crying all the damn time! Oprah had nothing on me! I was the ultimate crybaby.

I couldn't understand because I was happy! I was happy! H-A-P-P-Y... HAPPY! And every day our communication faded more and more. I started fading away from church, school, family, friends. I just wanted my baby. I didn't even want him anymore but I knew

I needed him for that. I was no longer in love with him and life because he started to smell of her and it was consuming me but I wasn't ready to face it. I just wanted my baby! My house had been shaken. I went from happy to sad in less than a year's time... I was no longer happy.

Woman on Fire
Circa 2006

We made a doctor's appointment to see what was going on. I didn't know what the hell I was going through and he didn't either! My hormones were indeed all over the place because of the fertility meds but that didn't stop what I was feeling inside about him. I knew I wasn't crazy but there was this stench on him, an unusual smell... literally. The scent of a jezebel, in my 'Christian, biblically correct woman that I was raised to be' stated. But my true inner self said, there was a bitch in my way and I 'gotz' to smash that hoe. Yes, I said it!

I knew I wasn't supposed to feel like that because I am a woman of God and women of God were supposed to be forgiving and understanding! We are not supposed to feel hatred and anger! We don't talk about the possibilities of another woman being in the forefront of our marriage. In fact, when I meet her, I am going to sit down and have a little talk with her and let her know that this is a Christian family and she has broken all of the rules... Once I found out who she was. In my heart, I knew something wasn't right, but in my mind I created this fantasy plan of how I would confront the mistress because I was a Christian. I'm getting ready to &*$% you up!

Woman on Fire
Circa 2006

By summer of 2006, things were different. Very different! He took me to Disneyworld, but he ain't paid for the trip. It was off one of those resort presentation gigs so this nigga didn't even invest in taking me on a real vacation! But anyhow, we went on to Florida, visited my favorite place, and tried to dismiss the fact that I wasn't happy. I was also embarrassed because my husband didn't think enough of me to take me somewhere. There was nothing romantic or fun about this trip. In fact, the entire 3 days were the longest, most agonizing days ever. I remember I tried to bring out the lingerie and have a fun   grown   up   night...Flat line_____. He made some excuse that he couldn't concentrate! I knew then, still, something wasn't right!

We walked the theme park and I had to go the restroom. I forgot I had his cell phone in my purse. I kid you not, this man followed me into the restroom with all of these other women to get his phone!!!! I was embarrassed but pissed. So

I pretended to not hear him call me and do you know he ran up behind me and yanked on my purse! I was like, "Nicca I gotta pee, are you freaking serious!" The little ladies looked at me like "girl, you alright?" I motioned back that everything was cool and I continued to look at him and told him that I will be back! I said "You can wait!!!" Honestly I totally forgot about his phone and was really in need of peeing! I threw the phone at him and he literally walked out like a child that just got his way in the candystore. We semi argued for about 3 minutes which seemed like 3 hours about his damn phone! He kept saying I'm sorry, but I'm waiting on an important business call! I was literally rolling on the floor, laughing my butt off. Really Nucca? REALLY! You ain't got no business! I knew deep within my heart, his ass was cheating.

Woman on Fire
Circa 2006

Things appeared to be good on the outside, but I was unhappy. He wasn't doing what I wanted him to do and now I was stressing my body which meant the meds would not be effective. He was dressing differently, staying away longer, wouldn't eat dinner, not answering my calls, sleeping with the cell phone! Lies, money missing from the accounts, unpaid bills, mortgage and car notes behind. The first letter of intent to foreclose! Are you eff'n kidding me? A what! But then a 9.9 quake shook 1772 Cedar Walk Lane! The foundation that had been established crumbled to teeny, tiny pieces. What in the hell just happened? Are you kidding me! You did what?

Yes, this was a 9.9 on the rictor scale! The threat of foreclosure and the fact that my eggs were not connecting with his sperm were becoming reality... Talk about shaken up! Summer 2006 was feeling a lot like hell!

Woman on Fire
Circa 2006

Still not understanding what was going on with me, the doctor says it was the hormones and I was changing. I thought she meant I was getting ready to go through early menopause! I started panicking big time. Hyperventaling at the thought of not being able to have a baby and I was only in my 30's!!! By now, I'm really praying, asking God for all kinds of miracles and blessings and help!

My house was feeling out of order. I didn't feel like I belonged there anymore. But I was still smiling and saying how I loved God and He is my healer. To the world, I was glorifying Him but on the inside, I was hating the fact that I had dedicated my life to Him because He still wasn't giving me what I was praying for. So the rebellion started to settle in. But I couldn't tell anyone that I didn't love him or Him anymore and now I'm sad. The fire started to spread like wildfire...

Woman on Fire
Circa 2006

Summer 2006, this 6'4" bald, once cute and sweet Negro said he booked a flight to Jamaica. So I was super excited! There had been so much tension with my being on an emotional roller coaster and sometimes bi-polar attitude. I was thinking that we were going to work this out, try to build us back up, so we were taking a trip to Jamaica... Together. I was excited! Really excited because that little trip to the theme park was a disaster!

I didn't tell anyone just yet that my man was taking me to Jamaica; I was getting my happy back! So I asked him when were we going? I needed to secure a substitute for the days (I taught at a year round school so we were in session). This 6'4" bald, once cute and sweet Negro looked at me in that guilty way and said "No, I mean I'm going because I know how much you used to travel the world and I wanted an opportunity to do the same."

Nicca, what da F*** you say?!

Woman on Fire
Circa 2006

What in the hell! What in the hell did he just say? So I took a long breath and looked at him, he looks back at me... I look at him. Dead silence! It seemed like at least 15 minutes before somebody said anything. I was the first to speak, "Ohhhhh, ok!" I said and I laughed my ass off! "So like this is one of those sexy games? Ok, I got you!" I knew damn well this negro wasn't playing no freakin' sexy games with me because he wasn't romantic! But I was like 'Awww, he really trying!'

So, my stupid ass, (yes, I was stupid as hell! I can say that now because I was) I really did believe that he wanted to play a game to break the ice so we could work on our marriage. I was praying hard too! Like, 'Lord, bless this marriage! Bless him! Bless me! Oooweee Lord, do this for me! Do this for us! I love him and I want our family to work! He is trying to rekindle the romance and surprise me! Right?'

Really I honestly did think that!! Serious black blond moment!

The day came... No packed bags for me but his were sitting by the garage door. Me:

- ✓ No updated passport
- ✓ No substitute in place
- ✓ Nobody knows of this 'secret' rendevezou
- ✓ No money

Hmm, Trinette... Think hunny! THINK GA'DAMMIT!

Woman on Fire
Circa 2006

I'm driving and he riding on the passenger side. Complete silence. I'm ready at any moment for him to give me some surprising details like, which parking deck was I keeping the car in? So, we pull up, my heart just beating. Stupidly anxious! Silent! Flatline_____!

I dropped the 6'4" bald, once cute and sweet Negro off at the airport. I'm sitting in the car. We were both quiet and even though we were at the airport, one of the busiest and noisiest places, you could hear my heart beat thumping with anxiety and rage. So I continued to wait like a dummy for him to say something like 'I'm sorry, let's start over, let's go and enjoy ourselves... Blah blah blah!' Holding my breath, I'm still waiting! Mind you, we're sitting in the loading zone. Wouldn't that be my clue that I ain't going nowhere because I am driving the car! Duhhh! This 6'4" bald, once cute and sweet Negro had the audacity to peck me on the lips (eww) and said "Be good. I'll see you in a few days!"

No exaggeration!

Woman on Fire
Circa 2006

I was in shock!! I sat in the loading zone. I could not cry, could not move. I just sat there and kept asking myself, 'Did he just...!?' I was pissed and felt extremely stupid embarrassed! I don't care what anybody says, when a man embarrasses you, you want to hide under a MF rock! I felt stupid as F!@&! My life was seriously like a mid-day TV soap opera! This was Reality Television at its finest! There was no script, no stopping the camera, no editing... This was the real shit and I had to deal with it!

What was I going to do? Pray about it? Man please! This nigga ain't got a pot to piss in, I'm struggling paying ALL of the bills & mortgage, car notes, and more and he got money and the time to go on a vacation! What the hell! I ain't praying for NOTHING and I mean that! I am done! No more praying! No more church! No more GOD! I'm done with this!

Woman on Fire
Circa 2006

I drove off trying to speed in that ole raggedy Dodge Stratus (drove it proudly) and headed to work. That should have been my other clue, right? I didn't get a sub so I had to go to work! What was I thinking? I wanted so desperately to save my marriage that I was willing to sacrifice my happiness and peace to make this work.

I remember sitting in the staff meeting after school, at my usual table with my usual folks. I blurted out! "He went to Jamaica!"
"Who?" They asked.
"I dropped him off at the airport for Jamaica."
"Who?!" They asked again.
As I tried desperately not to cry, I answered, "HE did!" In shock and outraged, they asked "Trinette, why are you here?" My mind was totally gone.. I missed the entire staff meeting as I sat in disbelief and embarrassment. At that moment, I didn't care about work anymore. I couldn't think, I just wanted

to get home and bury my head in the sand. My husband is in Jamaica with her and I paid for it... Literally. Status of Application for the show Snapped! **APPROVED!**

Woman on Fire
Circa 2006

Upon his return from his planned vacation... with her, I wanted to talk, get it on out but then he shut it down. Oh, so you want to be a man now and shut down? Hmmmm. Something ain't right about this picture. So we went to a local breakfast spot. I was too pissed to eat but you know me, I was going to eat! It calmed my nerves for the moment. My comfort was in the food which later became my best friend.

He couldn't look me in the eyes at all. I knew off the jump that he had done wrong. I asked him three times (that's my golden rule) and his answer was 'No'. Then after the third time, this nucca had the audacity to give me a stupid ass seashell and a size too small t-shirt from Montego Bay! It wasn't even a top quality shirt, nigga! Really! Really?! I politely slipped it back to him & told him to give it to the bitch he went with. I was so calm and cute with it. He looked at me, started huffing and puffing, eyes bulging, he hit the table. I sarcastically asked, "Oh no, you alright?" In my South Central LA state of mind... You just got made, mark ass nigga!

Woman on Fire
Circa 2006
Hot Grits Coming Through

So he became irate and hostile all while I continued eating my pancakes, eggs, bacon, and hash browns; chomping away in a sarcastic motion. Sipping on my coffee; knife and fork in a good position. Surveying my surroundings... Seriously thinking! He kept talking and trying to convince me that he went by himself. I kept eating... I don't waste food.

Please understand that there is NO exaggeration in this story.

A group of about 3-4 Police Officers sat at a table behind us, a few couples to the right of us, a big strong looking guy to the left, no kids in the area, all adults. Then my eyes went back to the officers. This fool was trying to cut a fool on me in public... Raising his voice, having a tantrum! But I swear, I kept eating. But he knew not to get too loud because you see, he's never known me so he is expecting the same Trinette that he played but didn't realize that he just opened Pandora's Box of unexpected wrath from this Christian Chic. The same Christian girl who was told to always love and not hate and this Christian girl was now filled with hatred and rage! This Negro had done flipped the script on a sista! Yes he did! Now he was ready to 'talk'! Ha! Gone with that bull'ish. But being who I am, I'm going to listen. My listening ears are now on...listening with hate and waiting to whoop his natural African American posterior. Hell naw... I was ready to whoop his natural nigga ASS! Yes, I was!!!!

Woman on Fire
Circa 2006

As I continued to eat, he was talking and the entire time as he was blaming me on the sudden distance in our relationship between us, I kept quiet. I was still surveying the room though. He said "You were so ungrateful at the theme park. I did the best that I could!" I was eating in fury and rage, thinking, that was your best?? He continued to lie about him taking the trip solo. He continued to lie about the missing money, his paychecks, and more. He just became an unbearable liar! It was sickening how a person that said they love you could lie so easily to you. Then he said something that really shook me! This coward of what was supposed to be a man said "You didn't do your job! You stay at work all night, you hang out with your family and your girls, you don't cook anymore, and you are boring!"

Ladies and gentlemen, I swear 'fo gawd', the pancake on my fork dropped as my hands started shaking! He looked and he had that nervous look on his ugly ass face! The Quiet Storm just arrived! I blacked out for a moment thinking, 'If I hit him with this pot of coffee, it won't really hurt him. And if I throw the hot coffee on him, it will burn a little bit'. Then I thought, 'I could take the fork and stab him in the chest, dripping with syrup and all. Or I could stab him in the eye, but I really don't like that look'. That was too gross.

So in that moment of blacking out, every which way of killing him right then had entered! Everything that my daddy taught me about men became real. I was ready to beat this nigga's 6'4" ass! I was gonna give it my best at doing so! And on top of that, I knew some people who knew some people who knew some people who didn't give a FUCK about life so they had no problems doing what I needed them to do! I ain't no killa but don't push me!

Woman on Fire
Circa 2006

The fork stayed in my hand and the spoon was frantically stirring the fresh hot coffee. The police officers were talking so I started thinking, thinking hard! And his punk ass knew it too! So I proceeded with extreme caution because I really do like my freedom! I really do! Lord knows I was burning with the desire to kill and not worry about being charged! But I believed God had those Officers in place at the right time. You could see some fear in his eyes but because we were in public and he knew I didn't like public nonsense, he had the upper hand in this conversation. However, it was God divine!!

Needless to say, I remained calm. It was like he said what he had to say and that was that! Still quiet, I paid for the bill, got up, got in the car and sped off with him in it. The drive was dangerously quiet and intense. I was thinking the entire ride home, why couldn't I hurt him? I was honest with God and I was praying for Him to strike him down! I was praying that God would allow me to hurt him. I just couldn't... Surprising thing, we made it home. I was still fired up and ready to burn the house down! He was scared as hell and I was too because I had never felt this fire in me before! What was I capable of doing? I knew I was capable of hating but didn't know I was capable of wanting to kill... Seriously.

He slept in a 'safe' place that night!

Woman on Fire
Circa 2006
It's a cruel hot summer...

June, July, August, and September of 2006 was the summer of hell! We argued, he lied. Money was missing from both accounts now. He was missing from family events, claiming to be at work. Little did I know he was setting up to be with his next concubine and the new family. I struggled to pay the mortgage and bills because he wouldn't contribute anymore.

Being who I am, I covered everything with a smile from Jesus and continued on, reciting scriptures about forgiveness. Even after the conversation after Jamaica I was told to forgive! But no one gave me the opportunity to really get pissed and outraged over this! I had to keep smiling, keep going to church, keep saying that God was good and all while I was dealing with my husband and his bull! No one helped me to fight this urge to kill! But how was this even possible? I was a church going Christian woman of God. How could I even think about this! My mind was enraged with such indescribable hatred for this man that I once loved. I couldn't see anything in him. He could have saved a bus load of kids, I would still hate him! He could be sick in the hospital, I would be there but I would still hate him! This is how I was feeling but I couldn't tell anyone that. I couldn't tell anyone what he did. I tried hard to keep my 'perfect' life intact on the surface, and all the pain hidden. My 'perfect' mind was exploding with fury & rage all the while I was praising Jesus!

Woman on Fire
Circa 2006

Our bedroom was defiled so there was no make-up sex, no holding each other, no kissing, no intimacy, and no love. He was not allowed to touch me in any way possible. I avoided him and he avoided me. The house was dead. He was still in denial that he went on vacation with another woman. He started dressing different, bathing as soon as he would come in the door (that's because he had her skanky scent on him) dead ass give-away nigga! And he stopped eating my cooking. Hold the jokes!

It shouldn't have surprised me because prior to this, I had been dreaming of an unknown woman for a long time. I didn't pay attention because I thought it was his brother's girlfriend or just some random woman. I didn't know God was giving me a warning... I ignored my gift of vision. The entire time I thought about her. Didn't know how she looked but knew that she was in my presence. How was this possible? I wasn't really sure if it were true or not but I knew there was a woman.

I was living with two strangers in my house. I had no evidence but the elephant was a huge one in the room. I wanted to know who this stranger was that had taken over my home. He had become a distant stranger and I didn't care anymore about him. He could have died and I would have been relieved. He was a stranger to me and I didn't know him. And now there were two strangers I had to deal with. Him and me, all because I kept that dream a secret. I should have listened to God!

Woman on Fire
Circa 2006

During the summer of 2006, I was a wreck. I still couldn't quite prove that he was cheating; it was really my gut and my heart telling me that something wasn't right. I started to question what I was doing wrong. I knew I had stopped dressing cute and sexy. I had reverted back to wearing my teacher clothes Monday through Friday, at work, at home and the weekends. I was so bogged down at work that I was closing the school with the custodians, so I couldn't hang out any more like we used to. I became obsessed with the baby process. I was placing my family and friends before myself and the marriage. Was he right? Did I become boring? The 'perfect' me was neglecting the 'perfect' marriage and the 'perfect' life. My life was in shambles and I didn't know why!

He managed to turn the emotional tables on me... Self-blame is the worst.

Woman on Fire
Circa 2006

Another season was approaching and my life was taking a turn for the worst. I started pulling away from people. Staying to myself and secretly living in anger and rage. I had resigned from a sisterhood organization that was no longer of interest to me and I really couldn't concentrate on being there for others. My sisterhood for others was depleted!

I was no longer happy! I didn't know who I was and it was painful. Still going to work and having to deal with people who were giving birth to multiple children and I still wanted to have this baby. I knew I couldn't have him touch me so trying to have a baby with him was out of the question. Feelings of jealousy had turned into true sadness. I started to put away Baby T's items, packing them in a small box. I was just about ready to throw it out! My desire to become a mother was fading in anguish and total pain. The marriage was dead and we were just literally going through the routine of keeping house. By this time, he was staying out all times of night, wanting to live a single life but reap the benefits of marriage. The finances, my finances were not in place because we, I, was hit with another foreclosure notice and I had to dip into my savings to try to save it yet again. He didn't care and I didn't either but I refused to lose my house!

I didn't know what had happened! Lying in the bed, night after night crying, bawled up. A depressed, lonely, angry woman of God. But yet life goes on...

Woman on Fire
Circa 2006

Mid fall of 2006, he wanted to try to work it out and we agreed to get some counseling. I agreed and started searching for a Christian counselor. We slowly started talking to each other but I was still on edge. I told him that I was coming out of the school system to pursue my dream of going full speed into business with my dear friend. He was ok and 'supportive'. We discussed the finances and budget and ALL of that! I was starting to feel different towards him because he was sounding and acting mature... Finally!

He still hadn't apologized and was still in denial about Jamaica but I didn't mention it. So it was confirmed that I would leave my job and he had my back. Business plans had been established 3 years prior, it was time to do it. I got some happy back!

Woman on Fire
Circa 2006

Plans were being put into place for the business and for me to leave the classroom. I was anxious, nervous, scared and excited! I was leaving my comfort to pursue a dream and I knew if I failed it would be my fault. I looked towards my family and friends but most importantly, I looked towards my husband for his support. At this moment, I buried Jamaica way back in my mind. I was keeping it moving. He told me that he had me and he played like he was happy for me. The baby process was fading because I no longer had time to continue to go the doctor. I had a few sessions left but the sex was off limits so...

Things were happening and I was thanking God... Again, He was doing it for me.

Woman on Fire
Circa 2006

November 2006 it was my birthday season and he didn't bother to celebrate it or get me a gift. That was so hurtful! My sister and girlfriends tried desperately to cheer me up and give me a private gathering. They didn't know what was quite going on but I remained cheerful and Godly and positive and all that jazz. Making excuses as to why he didn't get me a gift. I was in denial. It was the beginning of my lonely holiday season.

By Winter, he had downloaded divorce papers and placed them on the kitchen table. He couldn't do that because I just ordered movie tickets for the newest holiday movie and we were going! He started moving his things out of the house, little by little, saying he was staying with his best friend. Christmas Day came and there was a game. He wanted to go hangout and I wanted to go the movies I had gotten the tickets for. We argued, he got dressed in some new clothes and walked out the door.

New Year's Eve, I sat on the couch, mad as hell and sad as ever. I was watching the infamous Dick Clark Rocking New Year's Eve special when I got a phone call from him, saying "Happy New Year and I love you!" I asked when was he coming home? He replied, "In the morning." Yeah? Ok… Do what you do and get the fuck on. Happy Freakn' New Year to me…

Circa 2007

Woman on Fire
Circa 2007

New Year's day, I made a vow with God that I would rededicate my life to Him. I was sorry for all of the bull I was doing and sorry for not being a good person and all that stuff. I was lying because I needed Him to bless me on this new business journey and my marriage. God knew it and I knew it too. We all know that when things are great, we give Him all the glory and all the praises and all the halleluiahs and go to church and prayer ministry and Sunday school and Bible study and overdo it! But as soon as the world turns, we denounce Him in a heartbeat!

So I played the religion game for this year. I started praying, he came back home and wanted to try it again. I prayed and the finances were getting a bit better because he had a steady income. I went back into church full time because I was leaving the school system and I needed all the prayers and support from prayer warriors. I liked God... Again.

Woman on Fire
Circa 2007

The New Year was going ok. I had a few more visits to the doctor left so I went at the doctor's request. I was into it but not anymore. I had given up. With all the bull crap that was taking place, I was mentally tired and didn't want to try anymore. I remember my husband giving me a card, it said that I would be a mother, just don't give up. I thought that was the sweetest moment prior to all the mess. I started thinking about that moment and had a smile on my face.

We went to the fertility clinic and I looked around the waiting room. There were woman of all races, young and old. I remember seeing one couple come out from the back with their sonogram picture and crying with tears of joy. They were pregnant! That day, seemed like all the couples were pregnant and it was magnified! I didn't know how in the world this was going to happen because he was still not allowed to touch me. But I knew

~ **135** ~

he had to have sex in order to get her here. I just gagged in my mouth!

Woman on Fire
Circa 2007

That was it... I was done. Still not pregnant and I was tired of trying. Besides the money budgeted for this process was gone. I couldn't afford it anymore. I was sad, extremely sad. I had become depressed with a smile. I recall sitting at work and my school family would ask me what was wrong? I would muster up the words to say without crying 'I'm alright, just tired'. But deep inside, I was in pain and wanted to bawl up in the covers.

I remember sitting in the parking lot of school as I cried my eyes out. We had to sign in at 7:45 and it was 7:44 am. I didn't care anymore about teaching. I didn't care about being on time. I wanted my life to get back to normal! That year, my class was hell and I couldn't teach. Yes, that year my personal life interfered with my job. Sorry! I couldn't think or breathe without crying so how in the hell was I supposed to care for these children right

~ 137 ~

now. I think it got to me because I knew the kids cared about me and yet I couldn't even conceive a baby to care about. How could these kids love me and care for me and I'm not their mother? They depended on me to show them how to add, subtract, read and write and yet I couldn't even get my own shit together. Every day, for 180 days, these babies relied on me but who could I rely on. I tried hard not to 'love' them that year. I didn't want to love anybody anymore. I was a lost soul roaming the earth. I'm more than a teacher...

Woman on Fire
Circa 2007

I would look at her room and just cry. I looked at her clothes and as I started giving them away, I cried. I felt so bad. I felt like a total failure. I didn't feel worthy. I didn't feel like a woman. I had failed at giving my husband the one thing I set out to do and that was to give him a child. This one thing I had asked God to bless me with and He didn't even do it for me.

I was confused. I thought He said 'Ask and ye shall receive'??

Woman on Fire
Circa 2007

It was time. The last month of my teaching career was about to end! I was anxious, nervous, scared and excited! I packed up my classroom, used all of my days up to get things together from central office; I went to the doctor and dentist for my last insured appointments. I went over the finances and budget from my savings and annuities. Everything was budgeted! Even my hair and nail appointments for the next three years along with 3 years of mortgage and car notes. The plan was to pay off my car to eliminate one bill. The bills were placed on the budget plans. Everything was in place!

I was so proud of myself. I did it all by myself! I thought, I can do this with or without him but his money would greatly help! All I have to do is stick with the plan and everything would be A-Okay!

Woman on Fire
Circa 2007

He was excited about me leaving! I was excited! We were talking with each other in a civil manner again. I even let him touch me... Briefly. But there were no special chills and no breakthrough. I was extremely hot and I needed some release! You know that feeling of needing some?! Don't' act!!!

I was still not in love with him but I was learning to love him again. He was looking cute to me again and I would look at my ring and be reminded, for better or worse. I can do this. Maybe the business will bring us new beginnings! It was still something in my spirit saying something wasn't right. So let the faking begin!

Woman on Fire
Circa 2007

He was getting up happy every day, claiming that he had gotten a job with a railroad so he was in training. He wouldn't come home at night so I would call him and of course he was lying. He was at home with me during the day until it was time to go in to 'work' around 6 or 7 every evening. This pattern he started became routine. On the weekends, he was there most of the day but he was going to 'work' some Saturday nights around 10 pm. Hmm... Ok!

I had a meeting at the house with my Business Partner and he came in all happy asking for $900 for the dentist. He asked in front of my Business Partner who is a dear friend and sort of knew the deal. So I wrote him a $900 check, not thinking only to think, it's my husband and he was getting some dental work done. I didn't see him for the weekend...

Woman on Fire
Circa 2007

So the plan was moving right along. The Seed Sowing event for the business was scheduled and we all were excited! I gave the date and time for him and his family to be there. I was excited! The moment came and I called him all day to see where he was. His mom and grandmother had given me a lame ass excuse as to why they couldn't be there. He didn't pick up the phone, he didn't text, he didn't even come. The night that I needed him the most, he wasn't there. Not only was I hurt but I was embarrassed! My Business Partner's husband was there and so the anger and jealousy started to come about. Why is this happening to me! He told me that he had me! He told me that he was proud of me! He told me to do this! I really tried to hold back my tears as I explained to guest that he was in training out of town and that he sent his blessings and love to us. Lies! Lies! Lies!

I found email pictures of him with his arms wrapped around a girl... A pregnant girl.

Woman on Fire
Circa 2007

The baby shower emails/pictures had circulated to her family and friends. I responded with, 'Hello, this is Trinette, Mrs. Lewis*, his wife. Who is this woman with my husband and what event is this? He is very much married (and so forth). Please give me a call or reply back. Thanks and have a blessed day!'

No response.

I confronted him and presented him the pictures. He replied, 'Oh that's me & my cousin's cousin!' Hmm, Mr. Lewis*, that's funny because I don't see your cousin in this picture and we've been together for over six years and I've never met her. He continued to respond defensively and then his anger appeared! He was mad that I hacked his email! He must have forgotten that I was into technology and I could get into his email, phone, whatever the case may be... I could get in. It's a girl's thang!

He came home with a bag of pampers. I asked what they were for?! He stated that his mom was babysitting her friend's baby. He wasn't lying. He was her friend...

Woman on Fire
Circa 2007

I got a phone call from a friend. She was checking on me to see how I was doing since leaving the sisterhood organization. I told her that I was fine and just working on business. She proceeded to chat and then asked, 'How are you handling the baby and everything?' Scooby Doo voice… "What? I know I ain't seen yall in a while but I didn't have a baby." The phone became dead silent. She didn't have any intentions of harm and it was very innocent. She didn't know that I didn't know that all of this was occurring.

More messages were coming in about him and some girl sitting in *our* seats at the local dome. But then they proceeded to say that last season, she was there also. Another message came through asking how was the baby and how was I doing? Someone had called me and said that they had given him 72 hours to tell me the truth. I was like, truth on what!? DAMN can someone tell me what the hell is going on!

I attended a function where pretty much everybody from the sisterhood organization was there, including a few women he had dibbled & dabbled with. I entered into the place, looking as cute as I could but you could see the worries on my face. Still I kept right on smiling. The room stopped and stared and whispered. I kid you not. EVERYBODY knew what had happened except for me. I went to the bar to get something to drink and I overheard this dude tell another dude, "That's wrong man how he did her!" The other guy said, "Is that her?" I played it off with a smile as we locked eyes. Women whispered and a few in particular that I just knew he had relations with sort of snickered and had that stupid ass grin as if to say, "Hmmm, I had your man!"

It was like being in a movie scene where I'm the only one on the dance floor and everybody is looking at me! Literally this was happening!! I had never felt so embarrassed! But I still didn't have any hard core proof of any child! So what is all of this talk about? Why are people trying to hurt me? I've always been the nicest person to others, giving them whatever they needed and now this from sisters and brothers... Wow!

He came in from a game, all sweaty, anxiously trying to catch the phone calls that were coming in to me. He was explaining his side of story about the girl he was helping to change her tire. HA! My life was unfolding publicly and I didn't even know it.

Woman on Fire
Circa 2007

He had been missing for a few weeks... Missing from home but not from his family. His family knew where he was but didn't bother to tell me. I talked to his mom on several occasions and all she would say is "We will pray for him" and "Trinette, go ahead and get your business in order and just live your life"! What the hell kind of advice is that! Every time I asked her if she knew anything, she would say "He's a grown man." Damn Sherlock, I know that but where is he?

He would call me from a private or blocked number and tell me that he was in another state with the railroad! NIGGA STOP LYING! You've been working on the railroad for 3 months now and there is no money coming in, stop lying! He would then hang up and I couldn't call back. I called his homeboy and even he didn't know what was going on. I started calling all the hotels in certain parts of the city... That became exhausting. I started going through his emails again. This dummy changed his password by one letter!

Stupid! So I got into his email and started scrolling down... Montego Bay Sandals Resort Wedding Coordinator. I know he ain't trying me. Lord, Jesus, help me!

Woman on Fire
Circa 2007

American Express had been calling the house back to back and of course they weren't calling for me because I didn't have any debts, especially with American Express! So, I figured it was for his business and because it was in my name, I paid for the charges to keep my credit in check. It was well over $3,000! The young lady kept asking for him and I kept asking, "What is this for?" So she said she wasn't obligated to give me that information. I gave his social security and told her that she needed to give me something because she was calling my house with this shit! She transferred me...

So, I was able to get the Manager or whomever to release some very pertinent information. Of course I had to lie and I lied real good because they forwarded me the statements. Mr. Lewis* had an American Express card and had charges on there. There were charges on there for items in bulk for a Beauty Salon several times and the kicker... Sandals Resort for

two! I had paid for his and her vacation to
Jamaica!

Woman on Fire
Circa 2007

A year earlier, I had paid for his and hers vacation and didn't even know it until the Credit Card company began calling and eventually sent me the records. He was investing into this girl's business as well, but it was with my money! I kept looking through his emails and he and her had scheduled phone conferences with the wedding planner. Yes, the wedding planner. This bastard was getting married in October of 2007... We were still married and living together.

September 29, 2007 was the worse day ever! I died.

Woman on Fire
Circa 2007
Let it burn baby...

September 29th, 2007 I was getting ready to go to a friend's wedding. I was ready and happy for my friend. I still hadn't seen him and he was playing seriously with my emotions at this point. His parents were acting like nothing was going on. Lies were being told and I just couldn't handle it. I got dressed and I called his mother. She said, "Trinette, I need to talk to you, I will be over in a minute." So instantly my heart dropped and I knew this talk wasn't about going shopping. I was thinking, now you want to talk to me after I've been trying for weeks.

When she arrived, I was dressed and ready to go but I accommodated her time. I wished now that I had waited until after my friend's wedding because the news stopped me from attending the joyous occasion. She sat down next to me and I asked the ultimate question, "Does he have a baby?"

~ 155 ~

She slowly replied... "Yes, Trinette, he does." My heart dropped into my stomach and I cried like a baby.

Woman on Fire
Circa 2007

She wanted to hug me and I pulled back. I cried and yelled. My brother came into the living room wanting to know what was going on. I asked him to go back because I knew if I told him the full story, I wouldn't be able to stop him. Family is family and we stick together.

I asked how old was the child and she replied 6 months! I was in total shock! 6 months old and no one told me anything, including her and his grandmother! We go to church together and they literally live around the corner from us. We've talked on the phone almost every other day and no one bothered to tell me or give me a warning! His brother stayed with us for a minute and not one mention that something was wrong. I went on to ask questions and more questions only to find out that they attended the Baby Shower and was at the hospital when the child was born! What the FUCK! Are you serious lady! The ultimate betrayal from another wife, a mother-in-law, and supposedly woman of God! You did what??!!!!

She stated that she didn't condone what he did but he needed support from his family because he was the only one there at the shower! Lady are you fucking kidding me? You are condoning what the fuck he did! Somebody... Anybody... Everybody help me because I'm about to strangle this Bitch! Yeah I said it... B-I-T-C-H!

So I was right, the girl in the picture that he was wrapped around was indeed his new woman and they were celebrating the arrival of their son. It's time for you to go... Poof be gone!

Woman on Fire
Circa 2007

As I stared at her, eyes redder than fire, I was truly enraged with hate now for him and for his mom. I once loved this woman and had confided in her things that I couldn't tell my own mother and she knew that he did this to me! I lost ALL respect for her! She then proceeded to ask me questions about money that I had been given and more stuff. I politely told her that anything that they had given us, I never saw it. In fact, I told her that I'd been giving him large sums of money over the past few months.

So we were exchanging missing money stories and I was still extremely pissed at her! So she said, "Trinette, go ahead and sign these papers and move on from him because he has created a mess and I'm tired!" She went on to say, "I love you and you deserve more and better. Do you need anything?" Yes! Dammit! I need my husband!

Woman on Fire
Circa 2007

The visit from her seemed like eternity! She handed me a yellow envelope with some papers. This bastard had sent the divorce papers that he downloaded, by her for me to sign. His sorry ass was too much of a coward to face me so he sent his momma! That was another sign earlier in the years. He was a momma's boy! It was too late to get my contract back; my plan was crumbling all because of him!

I signed my name, Trinette LaShon Collier-Lewis* on the line. I didn't even read it... I just signed

No husband. No job. He left me.

Woman on Fire
Circa 2007

I remember after she left, I took off my dress and went into my bedroom and just fell onto the bed. I didn't have any strength or courage to even go to my friend's wedding. I was in so much pain! I couldn't bear seeing anyone take any vows. Crying! Crying! Crying! Asking God, what happened and why is He doing this to me!!!

I called my dear friend and told her what just happened. I couldn't breathe! As she tried to comfort me, I cried more and more. I just couldn't believe it! The baby I had asked God for, He had given it to my husband. He let him conceive a baby out of an affair! The more this played out in my mind, the more I became angry at God! Phone calls started coming in from some close Pastors and I politely let them know that I didn't want to hear anything about God and to keep that shit to themselves! I was beyond furious.

God had forsaken me and He knew it! I didn't need any prayer because I had been praying for God to save my marriage... So save that praying mess! I was done with God! Look where it had gotten me! Years of praying for a child, years of going to church, years of cheering for the Lord and this is what I get? Worst weekend ever! To continue this walk in Christ? I'll pass. I'm doing me now!

Woman on Fire
Circa 2007

It was the first week in October and he still hadn't come home but he called me. He cried and said how sorry he was and he wanted to talk. I nonchantley replied "Ok". I continued to search his emails and according to his mail, he was getting married later that month. Mind you, we were still married and I guess his plan for me to sign the papers had worked. I still couldn't believe it! All of the money that I had given him was for their wedding. They had guests and all! He purposed to her with a new ring, they had a home, they had the family that WE were supposed to have! She gave him the gift that was supposed to be from me! I hated him... I definitely hated her! He lived a double life and others knew. I was clueless.

Woman on Fire
Circa 2007

He finally came home, scared as hell! He wanted to talk. He cried and kept asking for forgiveness. Punk! Huge ass punk! By now, I was trying to concentrate on getting new business because I couldn't get my contract back. I was able to get a long term substitute position, at my old school, in my old classroom. So some income was coming in versus using up my savings... God, you are funny!

We talked. He confessed. He wanted me back and he was extremely sorry. I didn't believe him. I called the girl and her sister talked to me. They made me feel like I was the one who committed the affair. I had to ask them did they know that they were talking to his wife? She never talked to me because she was 'hurt'! Bitch, I'm the one that's hurt!

He told them a pack of lies! Wanna hear 'em?

1. I was a mean lady who didn't let him live his life...

2. I was an older lady...
3. We had been divorced for about 3 years...
4. I was keeping all of the money from the houses and not giving him the court ordered amount...
5. I didn't want any children...
6. I didn't like his family...
7. I kicked his brother out of the house...
8. I was disrespectful to him and his family...
9. I took their money...
10. I took his business away from him...

Lies! Lies! Lies! The frightful part was that they believed him because he had developed a relationship with them for over a year or so. I was in so much shock that as I was driving and talking to her, I almost hit a car! Now I see why they say don't drive while angry? He had tarnished my image and my name to the other woman.

Woman on Fire
Circa 2007

He deeply apologized for the lies he told them. He pretended to call her in my presence and tell her that it was over with! HA!!! Not going to work buddy! I know that game! After a day of playing games, he got 'sick' so we had to take him to the hospital. He was having seizures and wanted to die. Go ahead and kill yo self fool... It's ok! Do it!!!

So we played this sympathetic sick game for a few weeks. They prescribed his medicines which was perfect for me. As bad as I wanted to kill him, I knew I couldn't do it by knife or by gun but I could sure get him by overdosing him. Yes, my mind had gone there ladies & gentlemen. Because in the month of October and early November, Mr. Lewis* had created such havoc in my life it was beyond TV drama! I was embarrassed, I was in pain, I was out of income, I was losing the house, the car, everything! I was losing my mind! I didn't know which way to turn. I tried hard to keep my sanity and everything hidden from the public. The charade was unbearable!

He knew what he was doing and he turned the tables on me! He kept lying and he wouldn't stop. His parents didn't communicate with me other than to tell me to pray. What in the hell am I praying for and about! I told them to get the funeral arrangements together. He was going to die and I had every cause and right to make him pay! I don't give a flying $&#% anymore!

Woman on Fire
Circa 2007

Within a few weeks going into November, we attended my dear friend's birthday gathering at her & husband's home. All the people there knew him and now knew what was going on. He was playing that 'I'm having seizures and need my meds' role and I was still trying to play the 'devoted wife who is standing by her man' role. But there was indeed a huge elephant in the room.

There was a slight moment when he was playing with me, trying to break the ice and he pushed me. The men that were there, sort of stood up with that look like 'Trinette, just tell us when!' I had to give silent reply like, "It's ok... He's just playing. " My ex-husband thought he did no wrong. He was trying to make life continue to flow as though nothing happened. His words to me were, "I'm sorry and now it's time to move forward."

NIGGA WHAT!

Woman on Fire
Circa 2007

By mid-November, I had to let the house go because we missed payments and during that time, foreclosure was foreclosure. I was tired of trying to save the house, so I quickly started selling the items in the house from left to right. Getting rid of everything! The first item, the bed! We agreed on trying to start new so I withdrew some more money, huge amounts and found an apartment downtown. HUGE mistake! We moved from one expensive place to another...We could have stayed at the house. So we found a spot, put in the application and deposit. In fact, I gave him the application and deposit fees only to find out that he didn't place it to the apartments. So I lost more money as he continued to lie. He was still giving her money although he told me that they were done.

I couldn't fuss... I couldn't fight... I just had to move! I was on Red Bull,

Coffee, and 5 hr. Energy drinks in one bottle! I couldn't stop because if I did, I would think and if I started thinking, I would be enraged with fury and I just wanted to inflict pain on him. We moved in. You can't put old wine into a new bottle...

Woman on Fire
Circa 2007

My birthday, November 2007 was memorable; not with good memories but because it was the last time I had sex with a man... The last time I had sex with my husband. It was the worst feeling ever. My birthday party was filled with friends and family who were feeling my pain but again, that huge elephant was there. He purchased a Coach bag with MY money and tried to present it in front of others! Really! He was spending my money like wildfire! He didn't care. He still wasn't bringing in any money to the new spot so again, I'm struggling trying to keep my savings on budget. It wasn't happening. My birthday night was miserable but you didn't know it. Surrounded by folks who loved me and I loved them but I didn't love me or the man who was there masquarading as my husband for the moment.

After the celebration we went home and I tried to have a moment with him.

The thought alone made me nauseaous. The act left me with a taste like I had threw up in my mouth. It was completely over but I was hanging on to the love that was definitely gone!!!

Woman on Fire
Circa 2007

The day after my birthday was normal. I went to work and met new clients for the business. I was determined to keep pushing forward. Him? I guess he was going to work. Anyhow, a few days passed and I got the nerve to call her. This was prompted by the excessive texts and emails and pictures that were steadily coming through for him from her. I saw a picture of his son so I began to rage with pisstivity! Of course he kept denying that he no longer had anything to do with her... Other than his son.

I called her the next day and decided to talk to her. It didn't go quite well. She acted as though I invaded her territory! I never argued with her because again, I was the wife and last time I checked, wives had the privileges over hoes. So I listened to her and then she said this, "I don't know why you calling me because you ain't married no more!'

~ 173 ~

I replied and said, "Yes we are. We didn't file for a divorce; he got rid of the papers!" This is what he told me when he 'wanted' to get back with me. So I'm going back and forth with her about my alleged divorce. She then stated that my divorce decree was at his grandmother's house and she knows because she saw it so that they could get married. Seems like the more she talked I wanted to reach through the phone and snatch her ass but I was trying to be civilized! So I called him, he called her, I called them... He lied. He was still trying to marry her while living with me.

I called Fulton County, asked if I were still married. First time, the clerk, "Yes baby, you're married!" Then she put me on hold and checked my entire married name. "Baby, I'm sorry, you are divorced. It was filed the first Monday in October... You didn't know?"

She won!

Woman on Fire
Circa 2007

By now, everything hit the fan! He had lied about filing for a divorce. He had every intention of being with her but yet stay around with me to continue to collect money. He once told me that since we were divorced, I would have to pay him alimony!!! He better be glad God was on his side! What alimony? Funny! My money was running out! I tried my best to maintain everything once more. The apartment expenses were about the same as the house. We were just paying for location!

I would lie in the newly purchased bed that I bought, crying, but then I would look at him as he slept and would be like, "I love him. I want my marriage back Lord..." then I would hate him again. I remember waking up in the middle of the night, I went to the kitchen and got the long Ikea knife. I came back into the room and stood over him, crying asking the Lord to help me!

Finding condoms in his wallet, he'd lie that they were his cousins; I knew they were not for me... He was still e'ffn around with her. I'm so thankful November 26th, 2007 was the last time he ever touched me!

Christmas came and went. I tried to muster up some 'love' and got a gift for him. The purchase just ended up putting me in further debt. 2007 was my year of pure hell... Where was God?

Circa 2008

Woman on Fire
Circa 2008

A New Year brought new troubles! I could see things going down-hill but I was in denial. I was really trying to hold on but God was showing me the true Mr. Lewis*. The more I stayed with him, the more he rejected and neglected me. When someone no longer wants you, the feeling becomes surreal. Like, I thought I could handle the cheating and the baby but the fact that my husband no longer wanted me... That feeling was so painful! You fall in love, you love through the pains & joys, you marry and dream of a life of eternity, but sometimes just sometimes, it's just *your* dream. He never would look at me and definitely not in the way a man wants a woman. He was there for the money and stability of a residence. It was evident.

I found his camera and it was filled with their happy moments... Many of them. I saw his reactions towards her... I cried. Where did I go wrong? I tried really hard to be the perfect wife for him. Giving him everything I thought a man wanted and needed. I cared so much for him. And it was very public of how much I loved him and would do literally anything for this man. I changed for him. I changed for us. The vows that he quoted me were null and void. There was no truth to any of that. His promises were all now lies and his actions done out of convenience. I was tired by now. I was beaten; I tried to hold on some more but mentally, it consumed my mind. I was too tired to hate him anymore. You ever been at a point in your life where you literally give up? This was me... Right now... I totally give up. Whatever you like.

Woman on Fire
Circa 2008

I was told that they wouldn't be able to attend his son's birthday party. I was like 'Andddd, ok... I ain't giving a party!' This fool had asked mutual friends of ours to bring their children to his son's birthday celebration! Needless to say, no one attended. I felt good! The loyalty of some true people meant the world to me. But that shows you how bold he was. He didn't care about my feelings. He was so proud of his son and so were his parents. They wanted grandchildren really badly and I guess they got what they wanted... By any means necessary.

Woman on Fire
Circa 2008

My accounts were being dissolved quickly. I tried to balance and budget as much as I could, looking a hot mess while doing so. Clients were coming in slowly but not enough to sustain. He wasn't contributing because he had to now take care of this child. My car was raggedy as hell! He wrecked it, I collected the insurance money and before I could give it to the body shop, somehow he convinced me to help him pay his parents back for HIS debt. All $2,100 made out to his mom for... So now, I'm driving around with this wrecked & raggedy ass car that I'm still paying for.

The first notice was placed on the door! WTFruitcake! Fulton County... Eviction! I would leave him the money to get the money order. PAUSE! You'd think I had learned from before but I was trying to turn over a new leaf & let him be a man, because he said he wanted to start new. Bad idea! Resume...

Well, turns out that he wasn't paying... duh! So a couple of months behind meant, paying those two months plus court fees plus late fees plus ALL kinds of bull'ish fees. Mo Money! Mo Money! Mo Money! I was embarrassed as hell! You know people peep out the peep holes to see that big pink piece of paper on your door! The one that reads, "Warrant"! I'm an educated woman with 2 degrees and 2 businesses and I'm being evicted! Oh wait... I did get foreclosed too!

This started a series of two fights, both physical and verbal.

I tried to kill him again; 1 am, he put his clothes in a black trash bag and I dropped him by Georgia Tech. He was screaming and being irate. I didn't care and I wasn't scared... But when that Georgia Tech Police came by, I told him that I got this. He looked at me and knew I didn't want to go to jail but I will cooperate with the law. His punk ass got in the car and as we waited on our friends, I tried to beat the shit out of him! Good thing the local breakfast spot was available! I was tired, sleepy, and hungry! Food was in my 'calm down' zone. That night he was saved.

The other fight took place while he was walking in the parking lot trying to tell me he had to be security at a party! For real! What a laugh! No sir, you ain't going no where! So I ran over his foot and hit him with my car! It was his first time ever in my face that he called me a Bitch! Oh, so I'm a bitch now! Let me show you some more bitchness! I parked the car, took a shower, and went to sleep. He better be extremely glad I didn't punch the accelator!

Chile... I ain't finished!

Woman on Fire
Circa 2008

Sitting on the side of the bed, just coming in from running an errand and I was on my way to get beautified. Hell, I deserved it. Not having your hair done in months seems like beauty hell. I was just so happy that my mom had taught me how to use shampoo/conditioner, wrapping lotion, curling irons (them black ones you have to put on the stove!) and flat irons! Don't play with me shawty. And besides I was natural so my hair stayed in an afro!

I was on my way to the salon. I got my purse and had a little smile on my face as I walked outside. I usually forget things including where I park my car but I knew I parked it right in front of this building because my intentions were to run in and run back out. Well, well, well... I just stood there and a tear, literally, just one tear ran down my face. That red tow truck that had been circling the complex was for me! He waited and he conquered. He got my ride in broad daylight! Some personal items were still in the car but now it was gone.

I ran, that's a lie... I walked like Miss Sophia in 'The Color Purple' up the damn stairs, went inside and screamed! Screamed and cried! Asking God to give me a damn break! I was trying to go to church and believe in Him again... I just screamed! I was too embarrassed to call anyone but I had to call my friend and sister. I called him and all he said was "Damn, I'm sorry!" What? You sorry alright! You sorry son of a ....

Woman on Fire
Circa 2008

So now I had to depend on people to help me get around. I had never, ever, had to do such a thing! I've always had my own car and if anything happened, I had the funds or credit to get another one. My credit was shot to hell, my money was barely there, I had to get to the substitute jobs best as I could, I couldn't get rehired full time. No car, no money; I didn't know which way I was going!

I felt like I was losing it! Literally losing everything! I had nothing but my boxes & crates filled with my stuff, the bedroom set and my clothes. I never got settled in the apartment because for some strange reason I knew that I wouldn't stay. Another eviction notice was placed on the door.

Woman on Fire
Circa 2008

By now, I couldn't fake the funk in my life. I had to come to serious terms with myself and really have that heart to heart. I didn't get very far because I cried and cried and cried. My face was so swollen from crying. My eyes were always tired looking and red. But I didn't lose weight; in fact, I gained! Food had become my best friend and I did whatever to be with it!

I couldn't function among people. I withdrew from my family and friends. People would often say, 'I see hurt in your eyes!' No shit Sherlock! I'm in fucking pain! This is what I wanted to say to them but I knew they were trying to comfort me. I couldn't take it out on innocent bystanders, but he created this hateful undercover Christian monster. I hated life more than ever. I knew I didn't want to kill myself but I sure as hell wanted to run away and forget EVERYTHING!!! What was stopping me from running away? My family! Even though they didn't know the extent of what was going on, I had never been away from family so I was afraid to leave them. Resulting back to the death of my dad... I promised myself I wouldn't leave them. They didn't know this promise but I knew and I couldn't leave. I had to suck it up and go through it and take what was coming.

Damn! Damn! DAMN!!!!

Woman on Fire
Circa 2008

Without transportation, I had to ask for rides to church and to clients and to run errands. My sister would call and ask if I needed anything. Of course I didn't tell her everything simply because we are that type of family, always keeping secrets from each other. So I always said I was fine. I was secretly crying on the other end of the phone. He would leave to go to work every morning. I would be up 24hrs working so I would be wired! He would leave like clockwork to catch the bus so I didn't think anything of it. Then I started calling him as he was riding the bus but I noticed that I didn't hear others or that bus noise in the background. Hmmm... I know it's been a while but I do remember that bus noise! So a couple of weeks passed and it was the same thing. He would get to work in less than an hour or so, from the bus? He worked far from our location so there was no way in the world.

I received a bill from my insurance company (one I had been with for a while in good standing) and it said that I owe for this month's premium! $300! Mind you, I reported that I no longer had my car and they cancelled my policy. Besides I ain't never had to pay that monthly amount for a car! So I called them and the service rep (funny as hell!) said "Hunny, you got another car on this policy." I kept telling her "No ma'am. It was only my Dodge Stratus, silver." I gave the tag number. She said "Baby, you got another car on this policy." I didn't know she was hinting for me to really think so she wouldn't get in any trouble.

So I started telling her that I'm not sure what is going on, my husband ain't got a car. She put me on hold. I'm assuming she took me off that recording. When she returned she said "Hunny... (she stressed 'Hunny') think about your other house!"

PAUSE: Now, for those who really know me, y'all know that feeling of trying to give me hints and they fly all the way over my head! My Black Blond moment kicked in!

Resume… I knew she was talking about the rental property that I had but sold it to him. So she said, "You don't live there?" I said, "No ma'am it's now my husband's property." She cleared her throat so hard that I was like "Ohhh... Wait! Huh?" She told me there was a registered Hummer for that address and it was on my insurance. I politely asked if she could cancel the policy, immediately. She said she couldn't because I needed the social security of the policy holder and some other stuff, however being who she was, she asked me to give her a minute. I read off his social so fast! We were tag teaming on this! Sugar Honey Ice Tea… She was doing it and so was I!

We nipped that quick fast and in a flash! You riding around in a Hummer and I ain't got a car and on top of that, you ain't got no money! Nigga is you crazy?

When will it stop!

Woman on Fire
Circa 2008

I asked my dear friend's husband was Mr. Lewis* arriving to work in a car or by bus? He hesitated for a moment because it really seemed like a dumb question! How did I not know he was driving and a big ass truck at that?! So he calmly said, "Trinette, yes, he's driving. You didn't know?" I asked him what was he driving? He described that same truck as the Insurance Rep did. I be damn! This bastard got a truck!

So, he got home and I didn't say anything but I waited until midnight to go out to the parking lot. I walked the complex and bam! On the other side of the large apartment community was the Hummer! I walked up on it and looked inside; car seat, check, saw his bag, check, and his other bags in the back, check! The knife I had wasn't strong enough to stab the tires but I scratched the shit out of the car! I wanted to bust the windows out

but the cop would have taken me in...
Damn he was riding around that night!
I swear, the Police were Angels for me in
this season. They kept saving his ass!

A mature lady once told me that the
young chics like them boys with them
Hummers so be careful....

Woman on Fire
Circa 2008

I calmly walked back to the apartment with the knife tucked in, quietly opened the door not to wake him and went into the bedroom. I stood over him as he slept like the devil's angel. It seemed as though it was all through the night that I just stood over him. I thought he was dead because he never turned or twisted. I just stood there with the knife, literally, just stood there. No tears, no fears, no apologies, no doubts. I just stood there in premeditation mode...

Lord, please help me... PLEASE!

Woman on Fire
Circa 2008

I told him that I was going to kill him. He didn't say anything. He said he got the car because it was a good deal. Shut up! Please shut up. You're making this real easy to hurt you! Really! So I had to ask him to take me to the store, take me to church, take me to get groceries. He was feeling himself big time! I couldn't even drive the car! I don't know how he paid for it but it was his! Wow!

The time had come for me to call up my girlfriends and have a little talk with them. I planned a nice little 'Girls Night' but it was really my chance to talk to them because I had a friend who didn't understand the magnitude of my troubles so it seemed as though I had become distanced... I had. I called them over and of course there was crying after I told them what he had done and about the baby. Some could handle the news and some couldn't. Too many mixed emotions! Needless to say, I think everybody wanted a piece of him! They never saw him the same again.

Woman on Fire
Circa 2008

So much was happening! Another eviction but this time I couldn't get out of it. The fees were too steep to try to save it! I wrote a professional letter to management and explained but of course, business is business. Money was gone, totally! Every hard earned penny, nickel, dime, dollar and savings bonds, all of it was gone! Over 6 figures worth of savings & annuities were gone within 6-8 months. I was down to $200 in my account and I had to make that last. My items were packed and he said, he was moving in with his parents. So I asked about me? Where was I going to go? He said, with no problem, "You can go live with your sister." All I could think was 'Wow'!

In a single breath from discussing that the money was gone, he decided to go back to his parents! I cried like a baby! This was it! I was finally feeling this divorce! He lied. He didn't want me or this. He got what he wanted and he bailed on me!

I had one more follow up prayer meeting with the girls but this time everybody didn't come. One of my dear sisters arrived earlier than the assigned time. She saw me fight him verbally! I cared but I couldn't keep that image going of being a perfect Christian woman. We were calling each other names, I was throwing his stuff out over the balcony, bleaching his clothes. He tried to bleach mine... Tried. I cut up his stuff. It was just pure hate and frustration. I told him how I much I hated him and he told me the same! Nigga let me pack my stuff and put it in the car I'm out! I hope you and your baby die!

Please understand, that these were my thoughts and words back then, out of anger! By no means did I want a child to suffer because of someone else's mistakes...

Woman on Fire
Circa 2008

He packed that truck with everything I owned and hauled me down to my sister's house. I had invaded her house with all of my belongings. He just threw stuff in there! It was horrible! A week later, I got a storage and lost more things. The money I had left in my pocket, I gave to my sister for letting me stay. She didn't ask but I felt so obligated. I asked him for some money because he did have some. He lied and said he would help me! He didn't care. I was no longer his responsibility... Just like that, papers were signed and delivered and he was free!

My life would never be the same!

Circa 2009

Woman on Fire
Circa 2009

Another New Year came and went. I was totally depressed. Sitting in my blue robe from my grandmother day in and out. Looking for a job, creating jobs, applying for anything. I couldn't get back into the school system for nothing! All of my years of teaching experience and no one, not one were hiring! I was mad at God! I tried to pray but I couldn't because I didn't like God! He had put me in this mess and wasn't helping me.

I had to ask for help in every which way and that was painful! I became jealous because things were going well for others and here I was going through hell. I was embarassed, my life publicly unfolded in front of many and there was nothing I could do!

I remember, my sister would shop for her hygiene and household items. She would politely ask me if I needed anything and I would say no but she knew it. I needed the basics, soap, toothpaste, deorderant, tampons, etc... I didn't have a dime to buy anything for myself! How could this be! Really God, how could this be! I was homeless and barely functioning. Staying up all times of the night and day... Never sleeping. Broken in all areas! I was trying to get back into praying but I couldn't open my mouth to say anything to Him! God had forsaken me big time and I was angry! I lost it all! My home, my money, my car, my womanhood, my self respect, my dad, my business, my job, my husband. I lost me. I felt like nothing... I hated myself!

Woman on Fire
Circa 2009

He was in touch with me every now and then... Still telling lies. He gave me $400 one time and promised to give me more! I gave it to my sister to help with the expenses. I knew that her family dynamics changed because of me so I tried to do whatever I could to contribute. He never gave me anything else! I was able to secure work as a Substitute Teacher and I made it to the locations by using her truck. Barely getting there, I would run into many colleagues. Embarassed, I would often shy away from trying to say hello or talk. I just wanted to work, make a few dollars, and get the hell on!

Things were still seeming to go steadily downhill. The money I was making from subbing was being garnished now because of a bill from the marriage. So when people are depending on you to contribute, it hurts to give them more excuses as to why you can't pay. So more crying... No praying.

~ 205 ~

When I was not at work, I sat on that couch, in the same spot, looking crazy and a mess. I had lost my mind and I don't think no one knew. I was on the verge of a nervous breakdown.

Woman on Fire
Circa 2009

Late in the summer of 2009, I decided to try God. I had been going to Bible Study a bit consistently and joined a Young Adult Ministry. Broken as ever, I knew I couldn't do anything but come and listen and try to love Jesus again. I had to get there the best I could because I lived on the other side of the city but I made it.

I was feeling all kinds of ways about friends and family. I couldn't see the joy in anything. Not even in myself. My niece would look at me and I tried to smile for her so she wouldn't see me at my worse. She didn't know what was going on and I tried to shield her from knowing anything negative about her former uncle. I couldn't talk about him to anyone. No one allowed me to do so because they were angry. I couldn't even think about mentioning him. So all of these feelings were laying dormant in my spirit. I was still filled with hate. Every song that came on the radio reminded me of the hate or love... No in between. I couldn't talk about anything related to weddings or any of that!

I remember, when I found out about his adultery, I sent the wedding dress back to his grandmother (she had sewn it for me). I didn't want any parts of love and I was still feeling this way but worse. I just kept thinking, 'He left me'. He left me and he wasn't coming back.

The marriage was a shamble. My heart was black and a wall so thick had been erected that not even God could get to it!

Woman on Fire
Circa 2009

The year unfolded slowly. As I continued to attend Bible Study, I began to open up about what had happened. Most of the people there knew but didn't know the entire story. I still wasn't 'speaking' to God but I was willing to listen to Him. I had joined church and became active. I don't know why because I wasn't trying to do this again. I wasn't trying to get hurt following Him. He let me down before and had forsaken me so why would I want this walk?

September came around and we were doing a corporate Fast, The Daniel Fast. This is when I allowed God to come back into my life! For the entire month He revealed some deep rooted issues! MY GOD had shown up and appeared to me. His words to me, "I love you!" Tears were flowing from my eyes uncontrollably. I couldn't speak, I couldn't 'breathe', I couldn't see anything. I could only feel and it was something that I could not explain. It wasn't cold, it wasn't warm, it wasn't death, it was life and it was love... It was Him comforting me. What used to be a very painful and tragic month for me, September was now a healing zone from all of the pain of my dad's death and the death of my marriage.

Jesus loves me!

Woman on Fire
Circa 2009

I went to dinner for a friend's birthday at a local restaurant and again, there were people there. By now, I was able to smile a little. I had some income coming in from long term sub jobs. So I was ok. I was walking in and my Godbrother called me and said, "Hey, don't be alarmed but Mr. Lewis* is here. You ok?" I was like, "Yeah I'm cool." I brushed it off. I walked in, saw him, his mother, his GodMother, and his son. Our eyes met, his mother had this huge smile as though I was going to run over and hug her. He said "'Wassup Shon?" with a smile. I quickly threw up the deuces and kept walking; looking at his mom with hate and at his son with more hatred.

I asked God to forgive me about his son because he didn't do anything, but I didn't ask for forgiveness about hating his mom.

A few of my girls were igniting that fuel... "Look at him!" "You want me to cuss him out for you because we know you ain't gone do it." "We got you girl, we got you!" I knew God was delivering me... That was the last time I saw him till this day.

Circa 2010

Woman on Fire
Circa 2010

Working and working the business was going ok but it was still not what I expected. I was babysitting, teen sitting, and tutoring; keeping my focus on getting back on track. I was slowly believing in the Word again. I had rededicated my life back to Christ now but was still having some doubts. Even though He told me those sweet words, I was still having a difficult time believing because I wasn't understanding love and didn't know how to love. He was continuing to bless me with moments of peace, a little at a time.

Summer of 2010, I was just ending a long term sub position and I started to worry because that money was only good for a couple of months. I had again, budgeted my expenses for the summer. I was lining up summer tutoring jobs and babysitting. I got a phone call from a principal asking if I wanted a job at her school! HELL YEAH!

I didn't tell her that but I was very excited and at the same time, confused. Only confused because that meant I had failed at the business as well. So more mixed emotions surfaced but I wasn't turning it down because I needed a job, benefits and a peace of mind! Atlanta, I'm back!

End of story...

Woman on Fire
Circa 2010

I went downtown to Human Resources, skipped the interviewing process... That was all God! Got my hiring package and BAM! There it was! My income was the same from when I left! ALL GOD!!! The others in the room were starting from scratch! But here I was, the only things that changed were the insurances choices and my name! I was signing Ms. Trinette Collier! No hyphenation of any kind! Just Ms. Trinette Collier; no dependents, divorced, and I'm good. I was Hired! My God!

For 3 years, I had survived. No exaggeration! I survived my weakest and lowest points ever. An intelligent and educated woman, a woman who once loved Christ who lost everything including her mind was coming back! And I was coming with a vengeance.

Woman on Fire
Circa 2010

      Entering the classroom was ok. It wasn't this explosive feeling that I thought I would have. My focus was getting back into the swing of things, get savings going, and refocus on my business. By now, we had dissolved the business and we were now focusing on individual projects. I was hurt yet again but it was time. California Dreaming Events was my baby and it was time to relaunch it. So I set out to do things differently, reinventing the concept of event planning. I altered the moniker and made sure that my former last name was in no way were associated with it.

      Everything was going pretty good until I broke down in the classroom! My public nervous breakdown... What the what! Me? Nervous Breakdown? That's for crazy people, in Mental Institutions, not me!

Woman on Fire
Circa 2010

I was teaching and trying to email Mr. Lewis* about helping to pay the bills we'd created together, that were coming in. I never contacted him by phone but by email so that I could have proof for the lawyers. But it didn't work. I asked him if he would please help. Of course, he would give me every excuse and even had the nerve to think I wanted him back!

By now, I was back on track with Jesus, so I had to watch my reactions with everything I did. So on this particular day, the kids were all over the place (I had the worst class in the school) and the system/school was under a huge scandal so the environment was quite chaotic. I remember, everything went black and I literally saw stars! I sat down and told one of my students to get my partner in 'crime' from the other side of the building. She came and I stopped breathing for a minute. I couldn't see and I couldn't breathe normally. My heart was racing.

My head was pounding like someone was inside, beating it with a hammer! I was bleeding and it scared me because I wasn't on my cycle. They called for the ambulance... I quickly said 'No' and instructed them to call my sister! She got there quickly and quickly got me to Fayetteville! I was still panicking because of the bleeding and not being able to see clearly. They saw me, asked me that infamous question, because I had been vomiting, "Are you pregnant?" I replied, "No sir, I don't have sex." then he said, "Patient alledges inactive sexual activity, we still need a pregnancy test." Didn't I tell you I hadn't had sex since 2007! He looked at me and asked me to calm down... "It's ok!"

They gave me some meds to ease the pain. The Dr. determined that the bleeding was from the stress. He told me that I was suffering from migraines and he wanted me go to my doctor for more test but until then, they prescribed some of that good stuff! He also whispered to me, "You are having a nervous breakdown...

Let it go!'"

I had a nervous breakdown.

Circa 2011

Woman on Fire
Circa 2011

I took a few days off from work and a sabbatical from church. You see, after God had given me the ok to trust Him again, I went in full force, none stop. I started burying myself into work! People would ask me what I'm doing and my reply would be I'm working or in a meeting or on a conference call! I had to prove that I was ok and I was capable! I had to show God that I was worthy of living for Him again and I wanted to do it right this time!! I was on my way to becoming super Christian woman again. On another mission! But this time, I was able to find balance! I was no longer looking sideways or backwards, I was determined to do right. But first I had to do that very important thing... I had to forgive!

I never released all of the hate and disappointments and frustrations and all of the feelings dealing with divorce. No one told me that it was ok to feel a certain kind of way so I didn't know how to confront this myriad of issues! I kept EVERYTHING in, only to release tidbits at a time but it wasn't enough. My brain had exploded because I eternalized my hurts. I didn't know how to deal with a divorce. That was the second death to me. I had become very emotional because I still felt like a failure in it all. No matter what my girls said, other men and people... I, Trinette Collier, felt like I wasn't good enough for anyone. It was finally sinking in that he didn't want me. I had time to think and deal with it and I wasn't ready.

My Pastor had given me permission to take a real break from duties. I couldn't be any help to anyone if I was still messed up! And I was still a hot mess, a nervous wreck, still worrying, and hating him. Still dealing with the bills from the divorce that he got over on. I wasn't satisfied that I was dealing with all of this and he got to live his life, he got to have a relationship, he got to have a child that I had asked for and he got to let me go. I was living for Christ but still filled with resentment and anger over the divorce.

Woman on Fire
Circa 2011

December 16th, 2011, 11:40 am during my lunch break, he called me. After numerous emails asking for help, he called. The ironic part, my co-worker told me that I wasn't supposed to talk to him. She kept saying I was not to talk to him but I did. This negro was still very arrogant and stated that I was just harassing him because I wanted him back! Drop the mic! I had a few students in the room so I quietly gave him a few choice words! He then said, "Well, just file bankruptcy and we can be done!" I wasn't doing that again! You owe, you pay! Simple as that! Besides, he had the money! I was enraged with fury and it was my own fault because I had been disobedient! Clearly that was a message from Him above!

I was ready to let the healing begin... For real this time! That was the very last time I talked to him. Thank You Jesus for deliverance!

Circa 2012

Woman on Fire
Circa 2012
Unleashing the Woman

From 2010 until now, I have dedicated my life to serving Christ. I know it's Him and only Him that has kept me from killing myself and him. My faith has been restored in Christ. There is no magic and in fact the walk is 'harder' than before. I've learned many valuable lessons including learning to be honest with myself and God while on this journey! There is no turning back. I've learned to love again and that is the most beautiful feeling ever! To love another human being, unconditionally, that is God's ultimate gift for me... Love no matter what but through His eyes only. Only seeing the truth in others.

Each path is designed specifically for individual! My story is no different from any other person's. In fact, many may say this is 'nothing' compared to theirs and they are right. But what people don't understand is that you don't know your own strength until you are tested and I truly didn't know mine. That's why my testimony is my testimony and my praise is my praise.

Although I lost all material things, He promised me everything that I lost, He would give it back. Lord, My God, He has!! The blessings have been unleashed and are still coming! Mid 2012, I asked God to realign my body to where He wanted it because I had a desire to be recreated new. That meant even praying for remarriage and having children. He sent me to an OB/GYN and the process began. The doctor sent me through a few tests over the next few months. The reports from his office were awesome and divine! EVERYTHING was normal and in place... I just needed a man! You have to know him to understand his humor! As I left his office to go to the next doctor's office for the ultrasound, I praised God all the way! I felt good about going to the doctor to check my body for good eggs! There was no talk about my age or weight or any of that. I cried and cried and He said, "Stop that, you are fine! Who do you believe? Me or them?!"

Earlier in 2013, I had another appointment that was with the OB/GYN to diagnose the tumor that had prevented me from conceiving before. After a few visits and the treatments (running a special medicine through my system) the doctor came in and said, there's no tumor!!!! You don't have to take any meds but continue to lose weight! I stuttered and looked at him with tears (I told yall I was a crybaby), I asked 3 times… "You said I don't have a tumor?" I asked that 3 times! I can have a baby?! He said, "You sure can!"

For 10 years, I had been dealing with the pains, sorrow, hurts and depression of not knowing and being told that I wouldn't concieve but He promised me my daughter and I will name her the name that was given! Obedience…

PRAISE HIM! PRAISE HIM! PRAISE HIM!

A real breakthrough didn't come until I cleared out the storage that I still had!

Years and years of stuff still stored. Wedding photos and gifts and some of his stuff! I rented a truck, drove across town to Hampton and got to throwing that stuff away! Not crying once but thanking God for the deliverance! God was moving fast and He did what He promised He'd do! It took me a day to move out and the following week I got the news about my health! Release was everywhere! Obedience...

Remember that raggedy car that I lost? Well, God restored that! I was no way in any shape, form or fashion boasting about the car but what HE did for me!! From bad credit to my desires! It was all GOD!!!

Oh, remember all the debt? Over $300,000 worth? Well, although I didn't want to file bankruptcy again, I had prayed on it for over a year and God made a way! I really wasn't supposed to qualify for a Chapter 7 but GOD! I am no longer linked to him. He is completley gone! After the discharge, I sat in the parking lot of the federal building and screamed and cried the triumphant sounds of FREEDOM!

Praise Break!!!

My heart is opened and overjoyed with love for life, for people, for Christ! People always ask, "Why are you always smiling or seeing the good in everyone?" It's all God! My God restored me! He gave me the heart to forgive and the eyes to see Him in everyone. Even though my ex-husband pained me a great deal and I won't ever know if he is truly sorry, I forgive him and I send him blessings of peace. I forgave because I needed to forgive. If I had not, that stronghold of divorce, shame, guilt and more would have consumed me until beyond death do us part.

He, JC, Jesus Christ, pulled me out of this inferno of internal hell. I have a peace that I cannot explain! I sleep, I smile, I talk, I dance, I sing, I shout, I pray, I praise... That's what I do and you can't get me to turn back!

I know there is more to come because He said it! I now have high expectations of God and I know He won't fail me because He promised me! He won't fail us! I am a living testimony! I love God, The Father and He loves me!

Praise Break!!!

Yall are more than welcomed to call me Jesus' Girl, Jesus Freak, Holy Roller, or whatever! I love it because I know where He has brought me and where I'm going! My God! My God! My Good God! I am a Woman on Fire and ready... I didn't know my own strength!

Trinette LaShon Collier
Woman on Fire
Circa All The Time...
God is Good

This ain't The End

ACKNOWLEDGEMENTS

This journey had many seasons and in those seasons, God placed the right people in my life for that reason.

My parents, the late Iviry J. Collier and Carolyn Collier~
THANK YOU!

Aleshia and Aniya Collier~
I love you both and thank you so much for allowing me into your space! You mean the world to me!

Lucy Lu and Cupcake~
Keeping me company when Lisa & Aniya didn't want to talk to me ;)

Iviry, Bobby and Eric~
I see 3 Kings and I love you guys more than ever! Walk in His greatness!

Cameron Collier~
I love you nephew, even if you don't want to talk to me ;)

Sha'Von & Janine & Christina~
Thanks for supporting me all these years!
Listening to my Jesus stories ;)

Madea~
My grandmother, I love you dearly! God
has much in store for you!

Auntie~
Thank you for being obedient and being
my spiritual guide! I can't wait for you to
meet Mary!

My hosts of Aunts, Uncles, and cousins
and more!~
Thank you for your support and love as
family!

Robert Crawford~
My GodBrother...
Brownite forever! Love you dearly!

Mrs. Elease Saxby~
My GodMother from heaven! God knew
who to put in place to help me continue on
this spiritual journey! You are a praying
mother!! I love you so!
Thank you Gena for sharing ;)

Mrs. Gerald Crowder~
My GodMother aka Ma G! I can't express
enough, my love for you! I thank you for
always being there! Giving me that
spiritual womanly advice! I love you
dearly! Brownites forever ;)

Ms. Nezzie White~
My Spiritual Praying Warrior!
I love you!!!

The P.O.W.E.R Experience
Legena S. Crawford~
what can I say! You started this! Woman
on Fire! 2014 here we come!!! Love you
dearly!!! Don't forget to ask Jennifer for
the budget!!! MWAHHHH

Cosmopolitan A.M.E Family
Rev. & Mrs. Haithco~
You restored my faith back in the church
and God! Thank you!!! Love you!

Strong Tower Christian Life Ministries
Family
Rev. Jeffery Toson and Rev. Legena Saxby
Crawford~

I simply cannot thank you enough for what you both & all have done for me! You all are responsible for this Woman on Fire!!!! You are both more than just ministers, yall are people first and my friends! I love yall ALL SO MUCH!!! Thank you for believing in me and seeing the vision! Thanks for the space to host the events and more!!! I will never forget my STCLM Family!!!

My Sister's Alabaster Box
Arlene Korleigh~
Get ready Retta! We are going to be on fire!!!!!

Katandra Jackson
& the FreedomInk Family~
Thank you so much for believing in my testimony! I'm proud to be part of this connection!!! Love you all dearly!! Whew... I made it!!!

My Boyd Family~
I love you and I thank you for having my back!

My APS Family~
Thanks & Love ya!!

My MBC Family~
Brownites for Ever! Love you Dearly!

My STRUT Family
Darcova Triplett~
Thank you for this movement and
introducing me to Kat! Love ya!

My Social Media Family!~
Thank you for being readers & 'listening'
to my stories! I love you all!!

My SisterGirls
Our special names~
You know who you are ;)
Sapphire~Guess What! ;)
TeeTee~Thanks TeeTee!
Mink~Red room ;) Thank you chic!!!!!
Jas~Thanks for being a Prayer Warrior!
Jrae~You ready to create the Woman on
Fire Budget ;)
Tonj~It all started with social media!
Mika~The first woman who understood ;)
Erika~Woman of Faith!
G~Straight no chaser!
San~Thanks darling. West Coast forever!
LeLe~My sis... Little sis & don't forget it!

Kecia L.~Thanks chic for being there!
Trice~Seems like we've been praying
forever! GOD!
Karen & your five! ;)

To Mary~
I thank God in advance for you! I Love
you more than you know! See you soon!

Love,
Trinette

AUTHOR BIO

Trinette Collier is a 41 year old educator and entrepreneur from Los Angeles, California. She is the oldest of five siblings born to the late Mr. Ivory Collier & Mrs. Carolyn Collier. Being a military kid, they traveled and lived in different states, cities and overseas. Her father always stated that he wanted his children exposed to different cultures, races, and did not want them ignorant to the world. Therefore, she appreciated and valued her very adventurous childhood.

Trinette is currently an Educator with the Atlanta Public Schools system. She was blessed to receive her B.S. in Early Childhood Education from Morris Brown College in Atlanta, Georgia and her M.Ed. in Curriculum Instruction from Coppin State University.

Along with her formal career, she's also a Celebration Stylist in which she owns and operates California Dreaming Events, LLC. She is a very active member of Strong Tower Christian Life Ministries. Ms. Collier currently resides in Atlanta and enjoys being with her family and friends. She loves learning, spoken word, music, and dancing! Ms. Collier is very excited about becoming a published author and is looking forward to this journey!

The introduction of a new Imprint...

I am immensely proud to present this new baby (book) and to make a most awesome announcement! We have adopted another imprint. Yay. The family is growing!!! The suggestion was born of our own, Trinette Collier! Her exact words were, "Maybe we'll be under your new label of FreedomInk Inspiration."

My response, "Hey. I like that... Hmmm. Halo's and all that jazz!"

So of course by this point I'm on full alert. I'm in serious research mode. The power of words, the power of words... What to name this new branch? I'm looking up St. Patrons, Angels, Muses, Mythology, Religion and the search continued on and on and on and you get the darn point. So about midnight after a few hours of thought and research, I stopped. And I asked myself a simple question. The books that will be printed, released and published under the new imprint, what are they to evoke from each reader? What purpose will they have? And it happened. Doesn't it always happen that way? ' Woman on Fire' will be the first book to be published under FreedomInk's newest imprint, 2ii/2II! Each book's mission is To Inspire. To Ignite.

2ii

To Inspire. To Ignite

www.freedomink365.com/2ii

Happy dance with us for a moment please. I loooooove what I do. Yes! I am so in my element. Life can't get much better than this and if it does, well... I'm ready! This gal has been through the fire too.

Yours Truly,

Kat...

Katandra Shanel Jackson,
CEO at FreedomInk Publishing
www.freedomink365.com

Also available at FreedomInk

Angel Eyes: A Collective Memoir of Child
Sexual Abuse

Life & Love Through My Eyes

The Bride Diaries: Books 1 & 2

Loves Me Not Vol 1, Beautiful, Broken Me
Loves Me Not Volume 2, The Purge
Loves Me Not Vol 3, Miracles & Blessings

FreedomInk presents Poetic Meter &
Random Prose

Anybody's Somebody

Coming soon to a bookstore near you!

Dismissed Inhibitions
Good Things To Those Who Wait
The Lady, Niobe
Erotigoddess
The Diary of A Bride To Be Book 3
Rites of Passage

<u>Woman on Fire</u>

I was a very secretive person growing up. I had been taught not to tell my business to anyone. Whatever I went through, I had to deal with it and I did... Internally. My childhood was 'normal'. I didn't have abusive parents, no drugs/excessive alcohol, no mishaps, just the regular life of being the first born sibling. My mom taught me how to cook, sew, clean, be creative, and take care of people. She taught me NOT to depend on a man for anything! My dad taught me how to change my oil, work on cars, drive a 'stick shift', shoot a gun, start a business. He too taught me NOT to depend on a man for anything! That was my life from birth until the fire... Until I started smelling smoke. I began to think back to those infamous words, "Where there's smoke, there's fire". That's when I realized that I was already in the midst of an inferno.

Having the dreams of being an Entertainer, Educator, and Entrepreneur were my goals, in that order. But the most ultimate dream of all was to become a perfect wife and a perfect mother. My life plan was to have my name in bright, neon lights in my late teens and early 20's, marry by 26, have my first child by 28, become a Dr. of Psychology by 30, have my second child by 32, and one more by 34. By the age of 35, I would have been completed! Husband, children, home, luxury car, church lady, career (including an impressive resume), and more! I thought life was supposed to be perfect.

In 2001, I was close to my ultimate dream of becoming the perfect wife and the perfect mother. I married a man not chosen by God but by me. Although I was way off my life plan, I knew I could get on track with the marriage, but I had to go into overdrive to catch up! I couldn't wait, time was moving and my biological clock was racing against time and I needed a baby now! I needed for my life to continue to flow perfectly, because I was a Christian woman! I had been taught that you didn't complain or ask Jesus any questions, because He has been good to me. I kept the perfect smiles while enduring internal pain, hurts and depression on this Christian journey. I faked the funk that everything was alright with me because I had Jesus Christ on my side. I was a woman burning with the desire to become a mother and continuing to stay a good wife, daughter, sister, granddaughter, cousin, auntie, friend, colleague, and more. I was a woman not loving herself and realizing that she needed more; realizing that my life was indeed NOT perfect because I forgot to include God, on this Christian walk.

Woman On Fire is my testimony of how God changed my life through the rededication and restoration of my mind and spirit. This is not your typical divorce, ex-husband-bashing tale or a 'self-help' guide. I'm no expert on how to make your life better! Woman on Fire won't be able to give you 5, 10, or 20 steps to a more successful you! Woman on Fire will give you my testimony of how I went through the fire and came out shining like new brass; overcoming depression, feelings of defeat, being barren, divorced and shamed. Giving with my heart's desires a new meaning... To become a Godly wife, a Godly Mother, and more! He is the Head of My new 'perfect' life.

CPSIA information can be obtained
at www.ICGtesting.com
Printed in the USA
FFOW02n1605170317
33442FF

9 780989 678629